My Life
with the
Great
Pianists

To
John
Best Wishes
& God Bless You

Franz Mohr

My Life with the Great Pianists

Second Edition

Franz Mohr
with Edith Schaeffer

A Raven's Ridge Book

Baker Books

A Division of Baker Book House Co
Grand Rapids, Michigan 49516

To my wonderful family:
Elisabeth, my loving and caring wife;
Peter, our son,
his wife, Elizabeth,
our granddaughter Lauren
and our grandson Joseph;
Michael, our son,
his wife, Donna,
our granddaughter Megan
and our grandson Ryan-Michael;
Ellen, our daughter,
her husband, Gary,
our granddaughters,
Carina and Kayla

© 1992, 1995 by Franz Mohr

Published by Raven's Ridge Books
an imprint of Baker Book House Company
P.O. Box 6287, Grand Rapids, MI 49516-6287

Paperback edition published 1996

Printed in the United States of America

ISBN 0-8010-5710-8

Unless otherwise indicated, Scripture quotations are from The New King James Version. Copyright © 1979, 1980, 1982, Thomas Nelson, Inc., Publishers.

Scripture quotations marked KJV are from the King James Version of the Bible.

Scripture quotations marked NIV are from the HOLY BIBLE, NEW INTERNATIONAL VERSION®. NIV®. Copyright © 1973, 1978, 1984 by International Bible Society. Used by permission of Zondervan Publishing House. All rights reserved.

C*ontents*

Foreword

by Henry Z. Steinway

Franz Mohr has asked me to write a few words about this record
of his experiences with performing pianists during his many
years with Steinway and Sons, piano makers.

To understand Franz one must understand that he is truly and
thoroughly a religious person. His Christian faith is at the core
of his being and affects everything that he says or does.

Franz's principal job at Steinway and Sons carries the title of
"Head Concert Technician," and I would like to put this job into
its historical context.

Steinway and Sons started in New York City in 1853. From its
very beginning Henry Engelhardt Steinway and his sons sought
the advice of pianists in developing their piano and soon realized
that having their piano displayed to advantage on the concert
stage was very good for business. All the pianos in the world
today are made on what used to be called "the Steinway system"—a way of building pianos with an iron plate, overstrung
strings, a thin, sensitive soundboard, and other improvements
developed by Steinway and Sons in the middle years of the last
century.

Steinway and Sons has also done much to develop the appreciation of music in the United States. One outstanding and memorable event was bringing Anton Rubinstein from Europe during
the winter of 1872-73. He played 215 concerts all over the
United States, and with the Steinway piano showed a kind of
performance and music making never before seen in this country. Following this, Steinway brought over Paderewski for the

1891-92 season, with a resulting success which set the pattern for piano soloists right up to today.

In order to properly take care of these tours—the European artists as well as the many home-grown artists who emerged in increasing quantity—Steinway and Sons developed its unique organization known today as the Steinway Concert and Artist Department. This is an organization within an organization, developed in the last century by Steinway's incredibly gifted Charles F. Tretbar. Pianos are available in concert halls and at every Steinway dealer, each a nine-foot concert grand kept "concert ready" by a group of dedicated and specially trained technicians, who not only know how to service the piano but also how to get along with the performers who use it. It is not easy for a pianist to perform constantly in a variety of cities, on different pianos in different halls, and to be at the mercy of any newspaper critic who might not like his playing. Franz Mohr, the successor of a long line of head technicians, because of his expert knowledge and infinite tact knows how to help these sensitive musicians.

This book tells Franz's story. It tells much about what it is like to be famous and to play the piano in public. Not included is the loving care devoted by Franz and his associates to the un-famous, the debutantes—the ones who never quite make it—all of whom receive the same careful attention from Steinway and its technicians. Franz Mohr is a true friend of all musicians everywhere.

Preface

For years it had been becoming increasingly clear to me that I should write a book about the many people and adventures that have been a part of my life as a piano tuner. My wife, Elisabeth, has always encouraged me to this end. There are two other people without whom this book would not have been possible: Edith Schaeffer, author of so many wonderful books, including *Forever Music*, which focuses on the Steinway piano. Mrs. Schaeffer provided immeasurable help with the writing of this book, and graciously contributed several chapters of her own. And Stephen Griffith, with great understanding and skill has seen this book through its birthing process. In a way, I had the easiest part—just telling my story.

Many times I have called myself the world's happiest piano tuner. There are many reasons for my making such a sweeping statement:

- I love music. I grew up with music. Music has always been an important part of my life.

- I love the piano, particularly the Steinway piano. To me the Steinway is the best piano ever conceived by the human mind.

- I believe that God has made me creative and has blessed me with good hearing and other skills that help me work well with pianos.

• I find great joy in working with my hands; in hearing and bringing a concert grand piano into its best possible performance condition; and then in hearing this instrument under the hands of a great pianist in concert. This is great satisfaction.

• I love people. I have worked with all the major piano artists of my day. I have met many great people in my career—including every American president since we came from Germany in 1962.

• I love to travel and so does Elisabeth. Through my work we have seen much of the world together.

May your reading be joyous as you turn the pages of this book. It is my sincere wish and prayer that you may be greatly blessed.

*I*ntroduction

by Edith Schaeffer

New York at sunset time on a perfect day in May gives the thrill of satisfaction that many imaginations connect only with the Swiss Alpine rouge. When the red orange sun sets, down in the valley, the snow covered peaks and glaciers are tinged with a magic brush in rosy colors called "Alpine rouge" in French—seen from a boat on the lake below, or from trails as hikers make their descent, from villages like Gryon or Gstaad, or from the balconies of chalets.

New York's man-made Alps, the skyscrapers with their soaring lines, their diverse angles and planes, their gleaming glass, black marble, granite and buff colored stones, their penthouse trees and bushes moving in the breeze, are at sunset suddenly painted with the same magic brush. The myriad windows glow with red orange or pink. The architect's dreams seem to change shape with the unplanned touches of color.

Leaning over the rail of a lake boat on Lac Leman (Lake Geneva) at sunset, one's eyes turn from the watery glow of reflected colors to the windows of lake towns, the individual houses, the hotels, the Nestle buildings in Vevey, the sudden view of mountain village chalets, and one's mind tries to see beyond the walls and windows to the people inside.

Charles Lindberg lived in one of those houses above Vevey. Charlie Chaplain and Oona lived in another—"Right in there . . . that clump of trees." James Mason lived in another. Poets, writers, architects, actors and directors, painters, sculptors. Oh yes, Yehudi Menuhin is in one of the chalets. And Peter Sellers lived in another. Who else? The carpenters who build the chalets, the pastry cooks who make all the pastries for four o'clock teatime, the typists who type the manuscripts, the electricians and gaffers who are so essential to film making, the captains of the lake boats, and the men in the engine room. The people cleaning the room for tonight's concert in the music hall, and the men moving a piano in for the soloist.

People are behind the chalet walls, behind the balcony vines, behind the myriad glowing windows. People are hidden behind vines and trees, bricks and wood. People living, creating, having incentive and ideas, people weeping and laughing, people surprised by success and discouraged by disappointment, people cut down by depression or lifted by bubbles of excitement. Even if the walls, vines, windows opened up and even if a spotlight were turned on the people hidden from view as the sunset fades and lights twinkle out from the other side of the windows, it would still be impossible to know what was going on in the minds and lives of the people, impossible to know the hopes and fears, the fulfilled dreams or frustrated talents of the people whose faces one might suddenly see.

One watches as the lake boat stops at a dock and people get off . . . wondering not only who might be living nearby, but just who is depending upon *whom*? Which life is being affected by someone else not doing his or her work properly? Whose work is cut down by a sloppy partner or helper? There is that old saying about leaning on a broken reed, and the picture flashes into one's mind of a totally unnecessary fall for someone leaning on a mountain climbing cane. Which person is the "broken reed," not ready for his or her supporting role?

Leaving the dock, one sighs: How amazing that so much is going on so nearby—of comedy, tragedy, soaring genius, creativity, faithful plodding work well done . . . shut behind barriers, but also shut away within unspoken thoughts, unverbalized, unpainted, uncomposed masterpieces inside people's private minds as they brush your shoulders, or close the curtains of their windows.

And New York? Statistics of how many people and what

separate cities are contained within Manhattan's borders become impersonal all too easily. Walk along Central Park's trees lighted by that same sunset; stand with upturned head wondering who might live inside the windows bordered by grey sills or with views of penthouse gardens; look down the avenues and wonder again as uncountable offices rise floor after floor, and the mind boggles at how many actors, pianists, singers, dancers, are waiting on tables in the hundreds of restaurants. Who is living behind the sunset brightened windows, behind the walls suddenly romantic with reflected sun? Who is waiting in despair for a "break" in what area of business or art or performance?

To finite, limited human beings, too many lighted windows, too many people marching through one's imagination suddenly become a blur of merging, disappearing light, like a falling star blazing and suddenly blacking out, or a sunset glory turning to grey dusk. We may be momentarily eager to know—fascinated, interested—but we need to have something "cut down to our size" to really explore. One life. One person behind the window or wall. A few people whose lives depend on each other to examine, to study.

Books about people, biographies, glimpses into lives very different from our own give us the opening of windows, walls, doors . . . pushing back the vines and trees to see into other lives. People who live where we cannot touch them or know them, or even be in the same room. Though they live at the same time we do, in the same town or village, mountain area, or vast city.

Others we want to know through books can become friends although they lived in another period of history or on the other side of the world. What fascinating friends we can have, what incredible variety we can find, among the people whose walls come down within the covers of a biography!

As I arrived at the Steinway Company on West Fifty-seventh Street that morning, I stopped for a moment and looked in the windows, where the display of a few Steinway grand pianos with the gleaming wood (walnut, mahogany, or a special order of

white or black enamel) stood on Persian rugs in the midst of a
museum-like elegance. I stepped in, greeted Mr. Tupper at his
desk and Sarah at hers, and looked up with pleasure at the
vaulted ceiling with its wonderful crystal chandelier constantly
changing as the crystal sends out colored flicks of light, making
up for the lack of sunshine inside. The tapestries on the walls,
along with paintings, and the mosaics on the curve of the ceiling
increase the museum feeling. "What an unchanged setting in
the midst of a changing city," I thought as I waited for the lovely
elevator just to enjoy its mahogany paneled walls—even though
it is easy to walk down one floor to the basement.

I was on my way to see Franz Mohr and the other men in the
basement, on a very special day! CBS photographers were
buzzing around with their equipment in the hall at the wide
door to the loading dock, where pianos get taken up for loading
on trucks for delivery to concert halls. This was not an everyday
occasion, when a half dozen pianos go off on their journeys
across the street to Carnegie Hall, across town a bit to Lincoln
center, or to some other hall. This was a preparation to send a
very special piano across the sea! If a buzz can also be described
as a hush, there was a "hushed buzz" that morning at Steinway.
There was a quiet excitement, or an anxious air of calm. Over in
Franz Mohr's corner of the basement, by his special workbench,
stood Vladimir Horowitz's beloved piano—the one which for
years he always took out of his apartment, to go with him wherever he was going to play! It had been covered in the dark
green protective cloth, hoisted out of that high window, lowered
"carefully, carefully" down to the street . . . and received by the
experts at street level, then taken to the Steinway basement,
where Franz had worked on it in preparation for the long trip.

Ron, Ludwig, and the other technicians were listening and
watching as Franz gave final touches to the piano. To touch it
was to discover how sensitive to touch the keys are. Admiring
looks and differences of opinion punctuated the conversation.
Richard Probst, the Steinway Concert Manager, bustled in to talk
to Franz about meeting him in Moscow. And at that moment the
six men with the dark green cloth entered as if it were a piece of

theater, a play being put on for an audience.

However it was all very real. It was the preparation for Horowitz's departing to play in Moscow after years of declaring he would never go back! It was a momentous occasion indeed. No wonder each person having something to do with this historic event was a bit overwhelmed, with varied personal reactions. The legs of the piano were unscrewed—should I say "a bit reverently"? The men placed them where they would not be mislaid en route, wrapped the piano carefully, as carefully as a baby being taken out on a cold day, and carried it to the wide elevator door. We all followed. The CBS men were taking pictures for various newspapers as well as for the TV program, which might include this beginning of the event. Up we went in the elevator . . . and off we all stepped, not hindering the men who carried the piano out to the loading dock and the waiting truck—open with a yawning, mouth-like opening, ready to receive the precious load.

What a thrill to watch that instrument leave the building, headed for the airport, to be loaded on the plane flying to Moscow. How very "unreal" it seemed to touch the case, and to know that this same case would be unloaded in Moscow . . . and to hope that the concert could be seen and heard wherever anyone had a television. What expectancy of the impossible becoming possible. This was all before *glasnost* or *perestroika*, and it was a tremendous step for Vladimir Horowitz.

Horowitz had specified strong conditions for the trip. He would not go without his own piano. And furthermore, there would be no concert unless Franz Mohr, whom he always trusted to tune, regulate, and voice his piano, could go along. No one but Franz could prepare the piano for his fingers, for his touch, for his playing. "I never go without Franz Mohr going wherever I go, to properly prepare the piano for me right there."

This book is the pulling back of a wall in New York City, to look into the life and thinking and worldview of one person. It will take us back through time and space into Germany, through the walls of a little house in Duren—walls that were to be flattened during World War II with young Franz under the rubble. It will take us through his story of finding truth and certainty of eternal life in the midst of death and destruction.

Through the intimate memories of this piano technician who began his musical life as a promising violinist (until weakness of his wrist took that possibility away), we will also get unusual glimpses at artists whose music we listen to, whose concerts we attend.

Franz Mohr is an enthusiastic, imaginative, warm, responsive person who cares about people as well as appreciating their music. He has been described by pianists as "sheer magic." "Franz," said Mary-Louise Boehm (who is a concert pianist but also an expert on antique pianos and harpsichords), "is not simply the best piano technician in the world; he is a genius. He rebuilt an antique piano of mine which was a beautiful treasure, but which I thought could never be played again. When he finished, it had a marvelous sound, a beautiful voice." (Hand crafted pianos are individual, you know. Each one has a personality of its own, its special "voice." Pianists are sensitive to this, as it makes a difference in their playing.)

Most of this book has been drawn from Franz telling his stories in informal conversation. Each story reminds him of something else, so the stories are not sorted out chronologically. With Vladimir Horowitz's sudden death so fresh in his mind and emotions, he wants to start with the colorful Horowitz. He will give you behind-the-scenes views of many other pianists as well, and will take you into the world of his own childhood and wartime experiences.

As Franz and I explored the many fascinating details of the piano technician's trade, spiritual applications would often come to mind. Franz asked me to include some of those applications in the book. These appear at the end of chapters 8 and 9.

Accent, facial expression, eyes, and movement of hands make stories come alive! So you'll need to supply Franz's European accent and listen for his diversity of expressions as I attempt to turn his conversation into a black and white flow of words.

PART 1

The Pianists

1 Horowitz

For twenty-five years I was Vladimir Horowitz's piano tuner for all his concerts and recordings. I inherited that position from William Hupfer, who was the Master Technician at Steinway for fifty years and travelled with such renowned pianists as Paderewski and Rachmaninoff. Bill Hupfer was a legend. I began at Steinway as his assistant. He went to Horowitz's house once a month and took me with him, and then let me go alone.

I never saw Horowitz in those early days. He was very shy and withdrawn. He always slept late in the morning, and stayed upstairs when he did get up. As I worked on the piano, their distinguished butler, James, would always bring me a cup of coffee on a nice silver tray. He was the only person I ever saw, for months. Finally one day Horowitz came downstairs. He seemed to like me, and slowly we became good friends. He would sit on a corner of his couch, talking and listening to me while I tuned.

These were the silent years, when Horowitz would not perform publicly. During these years he did, however, do a lot of recording at the famous Thirtieth Street Columbia Record Studio, where so many classical records have been produced. I would go along to adjust and care for the piano. Many times I was also asked to turn pages for Horowitz as he played, sitting very close to him. That was always a frightening experience, for one never knew when Horowitz would explode.

If even the slightest thing did not go just right, whether his own playing or anything else that threw him off, he would go into a fit.   And *anything* could throw him off—even a dirty glass or dusty table in the dressing room! I was afraid even to talk to him, fearing I might say the wrong thing. I remember one day when he got so mad at himself because certain passages he was playing didn't come out as he thought they should—he hit the keyboard with his fist (and he is extremely strong), then jumped up and ran to the side of the piano and hit the stick that holds up the top, also with his fist! The top came crashing down with a tremendous noise.

Fortunately, such outbursts were soon over, and then he would become extremely calm. But he could not go on recording—he would have to stop and rest! Once when he had a fit of temper at the Thirtieth Street studio we rolled out a bed for him and he lay down for a rest right there.

Once at Carnegie Hall during a rehearsal, he yelled at me so angrily my insides were upset! He was always fussing around with the position of the piano, moving it this way or that, an inch one way or the other, upstage, downstage, sideways. And he was always opening the curtains a bit more or a bit less. He would try every position until he was satisfied.

That day at Carnegie Hall, he couldn't find a place for the piano that suited him acoustically. One of the stagehands suggested, "Maestro, why don't we move it while you are playing, and you tell us where to stop? We are enough strong people here. Maybe we get the right position then." Horowitz thought this was a great idea, so while he played the piano, some of the men moved his bench and others moved the piano . . . very, very slowly. Suddenly he cried, "Stop! Stop!" He thought he had the precise spot. Then everyone relaxed, and I went down to sit among the watching, listening people in the hall.

Unexpectedly he burst into a fit, yelling, "Franz! Franz! Where is Franz? I fall off this piano here, this piano is not straight. Where is Franz? Where is he? FRANZ!!"

I was terrified as I came running up to him, wondering to myself, *What does he mean by "straight?"* Beside him was a small table where he always kept a glass of water, and when he saw me coming he grabbed the glass and started to throw it at me. But then he stopped himself and it didn't even leave his hand. Well, we all walked around that piano and tried to move it a little bit this way and that way . . . just a fraction. We never did find out what he meant, and why he went into that fit. Something like this could happen without warning.

Horowitz was away from the concert stage for twelve years between 1953 and 1965. Then a concert was arranged for Carnegie Hall. Things were extremely tense. When a performer has such a tremendous reputation from past concerts and recordings, expectations run high. Horowitz's fame was so great that when the tickets went up for sale there was a line of people from the box office inside Carnegie, out to West Fifty-seventh Street, down to the corner of Sixth Avenue, around the corner and down the block—two days before the box office opened! When Horowitz heard about the long line of people patiently waiting to buy tickets, he sent concession trucks all along Fifty-seventh Street so that they could have free coffee and doughnuts!

Horowitz's next concert was at Orchestra Hall in Chicago. Horowitz always had his rehearsals on Saturday and played his concerts on Sunday. After the Saturday rehearsal, Horowitz's wife, Wanda, said to me, "Everything is fine for the concert; I have two tickets. Why don't you sit with me in the box on the first tier, so that you can be in the audience."

Like all concert tuners, I always sat backstage in case of an emergency. That night in Chicago was the *only* time I ever sat in the audience during one of Horowitz's concerts . . . because of what happened. There was always a great air of expectancy at any Horowitz concert, abroad as well as in America. There was always this electrifying feeling, with everybody a bit nervous. I, especially, would feel nervous about the piano. And I guess Horowitz was always the most nervous of all.

That night in Chicago he played a Haydn sonata as his first piece, after which he went backstage . . . and didn't come out again for a long time. I had a funny feeling already as to what was going to happen. Then the door opened in the back of the box where we were sitting. A stagehand stuck his head in asking, "Is the piano tuner here?" I got up and ran downstairs and backstage, which took quite a bit of time. When I arrived backstage Horowitz was furious. "Franz," he said, "I played so many wrong notes. Somebody has touched my bench. It is too high!"

"Maestro," I responded, "what do you want me to do?"

"Well, lower it!" he said. "Lower it."

"But Maestro, how much?"

And with his fingers he showed me about a quarter of an inch. So as the audience was waiting for *him* to come out, *I* came out, with a dark suit on; and people laughed and clapped, so I took bows as I walked to the piano and lowered the bench maybe a quarter of an inch . . . with the people still clapping! Then I went backstage and Horowitz came out and continued the concert. From that time on I never sat in the audience at a Horowitz concert.

Normally not much goes wrong during a piano concert, but I need to stay backstage for any emergency. In all the years I tuned for Horowitz, only twice did we have a broken string. Once during a recital at Carnegie Hall, in the middle of a piece, he himself broke the A-flat below the middle C. You could hear it go, with a big bang. Well, he tried to go on, but he couldn't—because of course the string was lying on top of other strings, creating a buzzing sound. I was backstage, so I simply went out and took the loose string away. That particular note still had two strings, so it would still play.

The other time was in Berlin. But I'll have to give you some background for that story. In 1986 Horowitz had played with tremendous success in Berlin. That was his last concert until two weeks later in Hamburg, so I thought, "I'll go home for two weeks and come back for Hamburg." I never will forget, as soon as I arrived home, coming in with my suitcase from JFK, there was a ring on the telephone. It was a call from Berlin! It was Peter Gelb, Horowitz's manager.

"Franz," he said, "you come immediately back because Horowitz is going to play another concert next Sunday. . . . Oh well, of course if you come by Wednesday, that is fine. . . . By the way, Horowitz made you famous just now. He told the reporters, 'It all depends on if Franz comes back. If my tuner does not come back, there will not be a second concert.'"

And I guess he did make me famous, because out of his remark to those reporters came an appearance for me on a television show in Berlin, shown on all the German stations; I was interviewed for a half-hour about my work with Horowitz.

But now we come to the broken string: In that second concert there was not enough time to tune the piano right before the concert, such a lot of things were going on. I could only touch it up a bit right on the stage. Horowitz's piano always stays very well in tune, so I was not worried about it. But that night as I was doing my final touching up, I came in my procedure to the bass section and discovered that somehow the whole section was too sharp. I had to go through and lower the entire section, one note at a time, as people were coming in.

Now, Horowitz had arranged a day off for the entire Berlin Philharmonic Orchestra, and there were seats arranged for them to sit right there on the stage for the concert. So they were already sitting there, and when I came to the last E-flat, there was a big bang as that string broke! Those musicians from the Berlin Philharmonic were more nervous than I was. I always say to myself, "Well, Franz, you stay calm." And I always say, "Franz, you have always resolved any problem that comes in your lifetime." And whenever such unexpected things happen, I always pray, "Lord, help me out of this situation."

That night I thought, "If I run to the box (we had a big travelling box with a whole set of strings in it) and take a new string out of that set, it will go out of tune during the concert." You see, a new string needs time to get stable.

So then I thought, "There must be another Steinway here." And there were—two Steinways backstage which belonged to the hall. I ran to one of those pianos, rapidly took the E-flat string out, went back to the stage and put it in my piano. The whole operation took maybe ten minutes! Then I begged the musicians and the manager and everyone working around the hall to please *not* tell Horowitz!

One should never tell any artist before a concert about any problem with the piano. He has enough things to think about already. But since I had taken a well seasoned string from another Steinway piano, the note was not out of tune. During the intermission I went out on stage and checked my piano, and it was just fine.

Many people ask me about Horowitz's piano. There are many stories going around as to what is so special about that one piano. I will answer that question very honestly and truthfully. Let me start with a story. We had an "international" concert one day a few years ago in Carnegie Hall. It was Horowitz's idea. He invited people from all over the world—with a special package deal with airlines, hotels, and concert tickets—to stay in New York for one week. Among those who came was a whole planeload of Japanese piano technicians, from the Japanese Technicians Guild. There were about 120 of them.

So here we are in Carnegie as the concert is taking place, and the intermission arrives. There were Japanese technicians running up with their cameras, taking pictures of the piano from all sides, some lying under the piano taking pictures there—all trying to find out what was so special about that piano!

Now I will answer the question: There is *nothing* special about the Horowitz piano! It hasn't been differently regulated; it doesn't work any differently than any other Steinway. The piano he used at that particular concert (serial number CD 314 503) was built in the early 1940s and was given to Wanda and Vladimir Horowitz by the Steinway family as a wedding present. He always loved that piano (although, as I'll explain in detail later, he also used four other Steinways during the time I worked with him). That piano was for many years in his home, and he took it on the concert stage wherever he went. About twelve years ago I put a new action in that piano, and also new strings, but the rest of it is the original piano.

Although there is nothing especially unique about Horowitz's piano, each Steinway piano differs from every other Steinway. Each Steinway is worked on by 400 different artisans and takes nine months to a year to complete. Not only does each hand-crafted piano differ from every other one, but they all differ from mass-produced pianos.

When I was in Japan a few years ago, I visited the Yamaha piano factory. I don't know the figures now, but at that time they were turning out 800 pianos a day. Each Yamaha piano is exactly like the other, because they are mass-produced. I have nothing against the Yamaha. It is amazing what they do. At the Steinway factory, there are about 120 jobs involved for the 400 craftsmen who are doing an individual piece of work. Each individual leaves his own mark on the piano. They are not machine made, just as personalities are not machine made. Artists know that each one plays a little differently, and that each one sounds different. That is what choosing a Steinway for an individual pianist is all about.

I look at a Steinway piano the way you might look at a family. Each child in a family differs from all the others, although they have the same mother and father. Each needs to be handled differently from the others. Each has different gifts, and we as parents need to see that we help our children to accomplish or perform in the area of their best capabilities. And so it is with the pianos in relation to the master craftsman, who will try to work with each instrument and bring out the best that instrument is capable of. I teach this concept all the time to my fellow technicians who work with Steinway pianos: Let the soundboard, let the instrument itself, tell you what it needs.

In the case of Vladimir Horowitz's piano, it is adjusted to what he likes, the sound he wants it to have. It is not necessary that anyone else likes this kind of sound. Horowitz always said that his piano had a little bit of a "nasal" quality, and he is right. He has worked with so many pianos, and this was the kind he liked best. It was regulated in the way he preferred. It has a very responsive action. That means that the keys go down with a light touch, there is no resistance to the fingers. And the "uplift" to their rest position is very strong. I balanced the weight of the keys in such a way that they would function the way he wanted them to.

Each piano is different, but each pianist is also different—physically and in other ways. For instance Artur Rubinstein would never have played Horowitz's piano. Rubinstein liked a piano with an action that had much more resistance to his fingers.

(But Rubinstein, like Horowitz, always insisted on a Steinway. I will say with great conviction that the Steinway is the best piano. You cannot improve on it. We produce a small handful of pianos compared to other manufacturers, yet 95 to 98 percent of the well-known pianists use Steinways. There must be something to it.)

When it comes to tone in an instrument one has to know what an instrument can take as far as "brilliance" is concerned. As a piano technician I have to see what each instrument can give me.

For instance, I cannot make every instrument which comes under my hands, every Steinway piano, into a big orchestra piano. It is simply impossible. Some pianos are born with a smaller voice. They are lovely, beautiful instruments, but not big orchestra pianos, on which you could play Rachmaninoff, Tchaikovsky, or Liszt piano concertos. Their tone is too subdued to compete with an orchestra. If I take a piano with a softer voice—one that's born on a smaller scale, lovely for a smaller hall or for chamber music—and if I force that piano, and build it up to make the tone more brilliant, there comes a level where the piano would fight back! That is, the tone becomes ugly, glassy, very harsh, unacceptable. The tone breaks. So I must feel my way very slowly.

Because I have worked so many years with instruments, I know immediately the potential of a piano—whether it was meant to be a big instrument, or was meant for a smaller scale. It is a misconception to think that the most brilliant instrument will carry the tone better throughout a big hall. That's a misconception many people have, including many of the artists.

You see, an artist is always filled with fear, especially when playing with an orchestra. "Will I be heard? Am I above the orchestra?" I learned much about this in working with Horowitz for so many years. His demands were so definite, and I wanted to please him, but I was forced into sometimes going against his demands, to protect the best interests of the instruments. I would stop and consider, "How far can I go? How far can I take the responsibility in working with a particular instrument, with the danger of spoiling the tone?" In chapter 9 I'll tell about one unfortunate time when I gave in to Horowitz's demands and, against my instincts as a tuner, was forced to spoil his piano's tone.

I have learned so much from Horowitz. As many of you know who have followed his career, he changed his tastes. You think about his recording of the Third Rachmaninoff Piano Concerto, in contrast with the recording of what he did on stage in Moscow—what a tremendous change. He changed his tastes and all of a sudden discovered Mozart. Yes, he had played the Scarlattis, but he had never played Mozart. Then he went crazy playing Mozart. "Franz," he said one day, "I cannot understand why people play all thirty-two Beethoven sonatas. Beethoven was a great composer, and some sonatas are outstanding, but not every sonata is good enough to be played on stage. Now there is Mozart. That is different. Mozart had every note in the right place."

Horowitz often made profound statements, and many have stayed with me. When we were on stage in Milan once, there was a press conference and he had a bunch of people around him, about two dozen or so. One of the newspaper people asked him, "Maestro, in your estimation what is the reason so many young pianists go into conducting?"

Immediately Horowitz snapped back: "I tell you what: There are no wrong notes coming out of the stick. That is why they conduct."

It is true that many young pianists go into conducting—Murray Perahia, for instance, who was a good and much admired friend of the Horowitzes and a marvelous artist. A few years ago, Perahia was going to conduct a concert at the Metropolitan Museum. Horowitz didn't go to many concerts, but he always went to a Perahia concert. So the Horowitzes were in the audience that day, when Murray Perahia was not only playing the piano but also conducting. During the intermission

I went over and said hello to the Horowitzes and Horowitz took me aside and said, "Franz, I want you to go to Murray Perahia and tell him to stick to the piano and not with conducting."

I said, "Maestro, you had better tell him yourself." Later he did tell him. Murray Perahia told me, "Franz, you know he is absolutely right; I had better stick to the piano."

Maybe I should say something about the five pianos Horowitz used during the twenty-five years or so that I worked with him. When I first took over, there was the piano numbered CD 186. (Every Steinway piano is numbered, on the instrument itself, as well as in a log book which lists every piano made, and when and where it was sold. Every Steinway piano can be traced.) This was the piano on which he did many of his recordings, and on which he played the first concert in Carnegie Hall after his comeback.

Then of course there was his own piano, CD 314 503. (Pianos from the Concert and Artist Department have an additional three digits, for easier identification.) This was the wedding present of the Steinways to the Horowitzes. He used this piano exclusively for all his concerts during the last four years of his life. Another piano he liked very much, CD 223, he used in his New Milford, Connecticut home for several years, where he also did a little recording.

Then there was CD 75. I will never forget when CD 75 first came under my hands in Steinway Hall. I never knew where it came from. As soon as I checked it out, played it, tuned it, regulated it a little, I realized that this piano had been used very little. It was built in 1911, and all its parts were original. It had just the right *spielart*.

I must explain the German word *spielart*, for which I know no English equivalent. Spielart means simply the way the action feels to you, or how the action functions under your hands, in combination with what comes *out* of the piano—the way it performs. An artist would say, "I don't like the spielart of this piano." He or she simply means, I don't like the way it feels; I can't control it; I don't feel comfortable with its action.

So I was very excited about CD 75, and said, "This piano has the spielart and the tone that Horowitz likes." So I called him and he came down to West Fifty-seventh Street . . . and fell in love with that piano! He played it for several concerts and took it to Japan for his first tour there, in June 1983.

Then he had CD 443 for his last four years in his home on Ninety-fourth Street. This is the piano he did his last recordings on. *Horowitz at Home* is done on this piano. His movie, *The Last Romantic*, was done on this piano, as well as, *The Last Recording*. I had wanted to show Horowitz this piano, because the moving of his own piano in and out of his house was always quite a production! At first he hated the new piano, saying over and over again, "Franz, that piano has to go. I can't handle it. I don't want it."

And I kept on telling him, "Maestro, the tone is already better than at the beginning. You are breaking it in—you can be very proud of yourself—you have started with a new piano. It is very good for your fingers. Of course it has a little heavier action than the piano you use for the concert stage—let me come and work on it every month." And I did just that. Finally he fell in love with it so much that he said at one point, just a few weeks before he died, "Franz, you know maybe I should take *this* piano on tour now. It is probably nicer than my own."

To me Horowitz was simply a genius. When it comes to the performance of a particular composer, another artist might have been just as good. For instance, I don't think he was a great Beethoven interpreter. I don't even think that he *played* Beethoven much. I only remember one of the sonatas, which he played once in the early years of my working for him.

I think a key to Horowitz's genius was his command of the keyboard. He had such tremendous color when he was phrasing on the keyboard. I know of no one else with as wide a range, from a super pianissimo which hardly existed, to a super fortissimo. I still remember when he used to play "The Consolation," by Franz Liszt. It was absolutely marvelous. He could change the mood and the phrasing in just a split second. He always played each piece differently. There was not a dull moment in his performance, nor in his timing. His phrasing was so absolutely marvelous that he never ever lost the flow, the moving of a piece. Many times his pauses were so far apart, stretched to a breaking point, before the music would go on. His timing was perfect.

I read an account of Horowitz as a young man, playing in one season more than seventy concerts during which he played some 280 different compositions, not playing any one composition more than once!

And he accomplished so much with so little practicing. When I compare him with other artists, who get up early in the morning, already putting in a couple of hours of practicing before breakfast, or the artists I work with who play until the last minute before a performance . . . never Horowitz! He *never* touched a piano on the day of his performance. He would even cut short any practice the evening before.

Once in Paris he was going to perform at the Champs Elysées Theater. Horowitz would go to bed early before a concert on Sunday. He had practiced a few hours on Saturday, but that evening we all went out to a nice French restaurant in a stretch Mercedes limousine. We all had a good time. Finally we were again sitting in the limousine after midnight, going back to the hotel, all of us in the car together, when Wanda in her quiet and pleasant way said, "Tomorrow you play your concert, and it is already very late. Why don't you go to bed as soon as we come to the hotel so that you get a good rest—and do not watch your two videos." (Whenever Horowitz arrived somewhere on tour, he would get a whole bunch of videos, and every night he would watch two videos.)

That's what she tried to tell him to do. But he responded, "Don't you tell me what to do. I'm not a kid. I know what to do, and I *will* watch my two videos." Which he did. But he was so mad. I can't repeat what all he said, but he went into a fit.

As we came to the hotel, Mrs. Horowitz shot out of the car and ran up to the hotel, up the stairs. And all this time Horowitz was very calm. He turned to me and said, "Franz, let's walk to the Champs Elysées. The air is very nice over there . . . just for a little bit."

So we walked over there and soon came back, and he watched his two videos. At that time he was very much into "wild West" movies.

The next day came his performance. The concert was a tremendous success, with a standing ovation from the audience. Horowitz's concerts were always marked by smashing successes and spontaneous applause.

Horowitz was consistent in all that he did. His rehearsal was always on Saturday at 4:00 P.M., his performance on Sunday. And I always had plenty of time to prepare his piano for the concert.

Of course Horowitz would have *never* stolen my preparation time in order to practice. He was, in that sense, very lazy! Over the years Elisabeth and I were always invited to Horowitz's birthday parties. October 1 is his birthday. Two years ago that birthday party was in the home of his manager, Peter Gelb, on Riverside Drive. When we arrived, Horowitz was sitting on the couch. It was a black tie affair; everybody there was well dressed (except James Levine, who was dressed as usual in his dark sweatshirt, sneakers, and a towel over his shoulder).

Well, as soon as we came into the room Horowitz pointed his finger right into my face, and shouted loud, so that all the people heard it, "I don't want to see you! You remind me of work! I hate work!"

And that was the absolutely truth. I never could tune his piano in his house before 12 noon, or sometimes 12:30, because he would still be in bed. Sometimes he would come down and watch me tune; other times he would come down when I was finished. Then he would have his breakfast. I believe he played a few hours after that, and then maybe late at night he played again for an hour or two. But that was the extent of his playing.

One day just a week before he went to Moscow, he came downstairs with a few people around. There was his manager, and Richard Probst from Steinway was there. Wanda was there, and several other people. I had just finished the piano. (He always came down the stairs well dressed. Sometimes I would say to him, "Maestro, where do you go?" And he would say, "I'm not going anywhere.")

So this time, I had finished with the piano tuning and Wanda said very quietly to her husband, "You haven't played that C-sharp Minor, Opus 2 of Scriabin, which you have in the program. You are going to play it in Moscow. I haven't heard you practice it once."

And he got mad. "I *know* that piece! I played that on such and such a date on such and such a stage" (he named a time some years before). Then he said, "Everybody *sit* down!" So we each looked for a seat, the few of us there, and sat down. And here was Horowitz, playing this beautiful piece of Scriabin, the C-sharp Minor, Op. 2 . . . so beautiful. Each of us was so impressed, so overwhelmed with the music.

When he had finished, he smiled that smile he had so often on his face, like a young boy. He cried out, "Didn't I tell you? I *know* it! I know it!"

Even Wanda was impressed. She said, "That was really beautiful, really beautiful."

Of course many of you know that recording from Moscow, which was absolutely stunning, absolutely marvelous.

Another time, I was talking to him on the phone while at work in Steinway Hall. I was looking at the Horowitz piano, which stood there locked up since no one else was allowed to play it. I said to him, "Maestro, it would be good if the piano would be played a little bit. Why don't you come down here once in a while and practice on it?"

"Practice! *Practice*! What did you say? Franz, how long are you working for me?"

"Maestro, I don't know, it must be six or seven years now that I have worked for you."

"And you don't know that I *never practice*?! It is always a *rehearsal*!"

Horowitz's lack of enthusiasm for practicing was fortunate for me. Since he only performed on Sundays, and rehearsed on Saturdays, I always had a lot of time on my hands. I had plenty of time to go sightseeing, and to do other things such as going to concerts, visit friends, and to do quite a bit of speaking in churches.

I always loved to speak in churches everywhere I went, whether it was in Japan, or even in Milan. We recorded the concerto by Mozart, the Twenty-third, and the Piano Sonata No. 233 in Milano Hall just a few years ago when Carlo Maria Giulini was the conductor. During the time Horowitz was playing these pieces there was so much time left over for me, because there were many days Horowitz did not feel like performing. I found a Bible church there, an English speaking Bible church, and they asked me to do all their preaching for five weeks. Elisabeth was there one week too, and we had a marvelous time.

People often ask, "How long does a piano last? How long can it be used for concerts? How old will your pianos get at the Steinway Concert Basement?"

In contrast to a mass-produced piano, a Steinway, which is handcrafted, in which only specially selected woods are used, will last almost forever. A mass-produced instrument is in its top performance condition when it is brand new. The factor of deterioration is very strong, and it goes only downhill. Not a Steinway. It is mainly the craftsmanship and the selection of wood going into the Steinway that makes it different. I believe with all my heart that there is no other company which is so selective with wood as we are. And since we build only a handful of instruments we can be selective. We are blessed with the best wood available. If you could only see the wood which is being *rejected* every day at the Steinway factory, you would be astonished.

Let me underscore this with a true story. It was 1983, the first time Horowitz went to Japan for performances. We took piano CD 75, the one built in 1911 which I described as having "just the right spielart." As soon as I came into the Okura Hotel in Japan, there came a knock at my door and one of the managers of this beautiful hotel stood there. "Mr. Mohr," he said, "I hate to bother you as you are unpacking, but we are so excited that you are here. We know who you are, and much about you, and we would very much like you to see the one-hundred-and-five-year-old Steinway we have in our ballroom. Please evaluate this piano. We just had some work done on it and we would also love for Horowitz to play on it."

At first I didn't believe him. I thought to myself, "Yah, sure." Then I thought, "With Horowitz playing that piano . . . we would never get him anywhere."

Anyway, I'm always curious about our instruments. So I went to that piano with them, taking my tools with me. It was a nine-foot Steinway. They told me it had previously been in Carnegie Hall. I copied down its serial number so that I could trace it. The Japanese technicians and piano craftsmen had rebuilt it in a most remarkable and excellent way. It was indeed a beautiful and fine instrument, in wonderful condition. A new one could not have sounded better than that instrument. I was very excited about it, so excited that I told Horowitz all about it. I said, "You won't believe it! Here is a piano, right here in the hotel, and it is one-hundred-and-five years old . . . in rosewood! . . . it's wonderful!"

Then one evening when we were all relaxed and had had dinner together, I mentioned the piano to Horowitz again. The ballroom where it stood was right next to the dining room, and we went over together to look at it. Horowitz sat down and began to play it, and exclaimed, "Oh that is beautiful, beautiful! Why did I bring *my* piano? I could play the concert on this one!" He played Vienna waltzes and said, "Dance, dance, dance!" It was such a special evening.

A hand-crafted piano like this will go on forever and ever if you handle it right. This is something you could never get from a mass-produced instrument.

Unfortunately that Japan tour of June 1983 was a disaster. Horowitz was physically in very bad shape. He could not sleep, and he took a lot of pills. Just before we went to Japan, when we had several concerts here—Boston, Chicago, Cleveland and so on—he was having physical problems. There was a young doctor who travelled with us all the time. Horowitz would take extended breaks, and extended intermissions of even thirty-five or forty minutes, during which the doctor would go over him. I never trusted that doctor, and I don't know his name, but he would dope Horowitz up so much that he was not able to control his fingers, and he played a terrible concert there in Japan.

He knew he hadn't done well. After the concert he sat there in his chair, totally exhausted, hardly able to speak, and said, "I know . . . lots of wrong notes . . . lots of wrong notes. . . . I don't know what is happening to me."

Meanwhile Wanda was crying on my shoulder, and she said, "Franz, Franz, this today was a funeral. This was a funeral. We will never hear Horowitz again. He was terrible. Absolutely terrible."

We all feared it was true—that we would never hear him again. There followed three months of quietness in his home. I never saw him during those three months, even though I came by each month to tune his piano. Then one day he came down, just like in the old days, all dressed up. And the first thing he said to me was, "Franz, you must know: I don't take anything anymore. No longer do I use my body as a garbage pail. I am not even taking sleeping pills anymore. And you know what? I am going to play! And I show the world that I can still play the piano."

And he did come back. All the rest of his concerts and tours were tremendous successes. One of the most memorable was the one in Russia, on April 20, 1986. I'll never forget the Saturday rehearsal for the Moscow concert. Horowitz had heard that the students from the conservatory had not been able to get any tickets for the concert on Sunday; he was moved by this, and invited all of them to come to the rehearsal. Then he played a real concert for the students. I have it on video tape. You can see many of the students in tears as they listen to Horowitz.

There is so much to tell about our three weeks in Russia. I will save most of it for another chapter.

The last time Horowitz recorded was on November 1, 1989. It was a Wednesday. We were at his home, and he did very well. But I must tell you this story. Here is the recording project, set up in his home, and there is Horowitz sitting at his piano, with Mordecai Shehori standing next to him turning pages. Mordecai Shehori is a wonderful Israeli pianist, a good friend of the

Horowitzes and a good friend of mine too. I was sitting where I usually sat, in the corner of that big couch, being very quiet, not making a sound, just being excited in watching Horowitz as he performed so well. Tom Frost, the producer, and Tom Lazarus, the technician, were in another room of the house, directing the recording from there.

It was maybe a week before that Horowitz had bought himself a very expensive watch, and he had it on that day. He was very proud of that watch. He had showed it to everyone saying, "Look at this, just look at this! Ten thousand dollars!" He said this to everyone. Sometimes he was like a child. Oh, but he was proud of that new watch.

He was playing a Chopin etude. As he came to the last arpeggio, which he played up to the treble, he paused (as I said, his timing was always perfect) . . . and *just* before the last chord on the piano, he stopped, looked at his watch, showed it to me, smiled happily—very proud of the watch on his wrist—and then . . . just in time . . . came the last chord—perfectly! I am saying that his timing was absolutely perfect, always.

And yet, Horowitz had no control whatsoever as to the timing of his death—even though he was at that time very much in control of his physical body. The last few years he took extremely good care of himself. He slept a lot, exercised by walking every day, and was careful in what he ate. All his life, in fact, the only meat he would eat was fish or chicken. When we were in Russia, the Dover sole he liked had to be flown in every day. Several years before his death he had given up smoking completely, and he would not even drink any wine or alcohol. He took very good care, but the timing of his death was out of his control.

It was just as in Hebrews 9:27, where it says, "It is appointed for men to die once, and after this the judgment." And it is very sad that although I had opportunity a few times to talk to Horowitz about the Lord, about salvation, yet as far as I know, there was never any real breakthrough where with assurance I could say that he believed, and knew where he would be going after death.

After the recording session that last Wednesday, Horowitz was very relaxed, and everybody was happy because it had gone so well. So we were all sitting together in his music room where his big piano was, where the recording had taken place. There was tea served, with cookies for all of us. Mordecai Shehori turned to Horowitz and said, "You know, Maestro, you are really blessed. Your fingers move very well, you are playing so well as never before, and you have friends here who love you very much and who pray for you all the time."

Just then Horowitz interjected and said, "Oh, have you ever heard Franz pray? He prays so beautiful . . . you must hear it. I have heard him pray in his home, and one day I asked him to pray with us in Japan."

That was the only reference which he made concerning spiritual matters that day, before his death the following Sunday.

When I now think back, I am sorry that I didn't stay longer that night and look for an opportunity to talk about eternal life and our Lord Jesus Christ. But at one point during that evening, Tom Frost said, "Did you read in the paper that Malcolm Forbes gave his birthday party, which cost him a million dollars, and he was very proud of it. It was in the paper. And did you read too that when one of the reporters who was interviewing him asked this question, 'If you could have one wish, what would it be?' . . . he said immediately, 'I want eternal life; what I desire is immortality in a healthy body.'"

At this point I said, while everybody was there, "And you know what? Everyone *can* have this for the asking!"

And there was no response from any of them. It went over everyone's head. Nobody understood what I was trying to say. So . . . that is all I said. I'm always looking for an opening, an opportunity to speak of the important things . . . but at that time, that was all I said.

At that time I was very tired. The night before we had had a concert in Carnegie Hall, so I was tired and anxious to start the long drive home, so I said, "May I be excused? I really would like to go home."

Everybody stayed on. I left while they were still talking and enjoying themselves. But now I am so sorry I didn't stay longer, looking for the right opening to speak of the gospel of our Lord Jesus Christ with all those people that night.

I came to the Horowitz home for the next recording session on that Friday, but Horowitz didn't feel well, so the session had been cancelled. I did not see him on Friday at all. "The next session will be on Monday," I was told, "because Horowitz has a cold and doesn't feel well."

So I went back to Steinway. Later Wanda told me, "He didn't feel well on Friday and said, 'I don't know if it is a cold.' With his hands and fingertips he touched his upper shoulder on both sides and said, 'I don't know, but it hurts up here; I don't know what it is.' So I said, 'Well, let's ask the doctor.' So I made an appointment, and the doctor came on Saturday and checked him out. At the end the doctor said, 'Horowitz, you have the heart of a young man. You are fine. You just have a cold, but you will be fine in a few days. Just rest.' He slept very well that night— Saturday night to Sunday morning."

There were plans for Murray Perahia to go out for dinner with them on Sunday. He was supposed to come to the house Sunday afternoon, and then they would go out for dinner. Wanda and Horowitz were sitting on the couch together making plans for where they would go, and what they would eat, and just what they would order from the chef. Wanda was taking notes. They had planned to go to one of the restaurants where they are very well known, and where they go frequently. In the middle of Wanda's note taking, as they were saying that Murray Perahia would be there in an hour or so, and they must finally decide about the dinner menu, all of a sudden Horowitz leaned back, with his head on the back of the couch, and breathed his last breath.

Wanda told me, "I knew that he had died. We called 911, and they were there within a few minutes. They worked on him there on the couch for a whole hour. But I knew they could not and would not revive him. I knew that he was dead."

That was Sunday, during the time when Elisabeth, Ellen, Gary, and I were in church. When we got home we saw that there was a message in the machine. As I listened to the message it was Juliana, a personal assistant to Horowitz and his wife, calling from the Horowitz home saying, "Please call, Franz, call the Horowitz home. It's an emergency." I knew something had happened, and that it was very serious. I thought, "Something has happened to Horowitz." As I called, it was Wanda who answered and, when she heard my voice she started to cry, and said, "Horowitz is dead. Horowitz is dead."

Well, I was terribly moved by his sudden death. Many people said it was a real blessing that he went that way, without pain, without suffering. True. But sometimes, it might be good for certain people to have a time of grace, so to speak, when they are warned very definitely about the approach of their death— a time when they can "set their house in order," and, much more impotantly, when they can make a decision for the Lord Jesus Christ.

However what I want to speak about now is positive. I want to tell you a couple of stories of times when I was able to speak with the Horowitzes about my faith. All through the years I prayed often for Horowitz. But the very first time I could speak to Horowitz about my faith was a definite answer to prayer. I had already worked for him for many years, and one year the first concert of the season was on the stage of the concert hall in Rochester, New York. When the stagehand was about to open the door for Horowitz to go out and perform, just before he stepped out to face the audience and his piano, he turned to me and said, "Franz, out there is the loneliest place in the world."

You know, at that very moment when Horowitz walked out on the stage, as I watched him, all of a sudden in my heart I responded to his statement and thought, *Horowitz, if you only would know what the loneliest place in the history of mankind ever was.* I thought about the crucifixion of our Lord, when he was forsaken, not only by his friends, his disciples, but even by his heavenly Father, so that he had to cry out, "My God, my God, why hast thou forsaken me?" And of course it was because the Lord Jesus was made sin for us ("He who knew no sin became sin for us"); that was why the heavenly Father had to turn away from him. And he died in utter loneliness, having the greatest pain he ever could have experienced, being forsaken by his heavenly Father.

So I thought, *Well, Horowitz, I never talked to you about all this*, and right there, standing backstage in Rochester, New York, that night, I prayed, "Please, Lord, open the door, that somehow the circumstances will be such that I can talk to Horowitz about you some day."

The door was opened the following weekend. As I told you, Horowitz only played once a week, on Sunday. The following week we went to Boston. Horowitz was at the Prudential Center in the Sheraton. While he was in his suite, playing on the piano, one of the notes would not perform properly for him. There were several people there in his suite, among them David Rubin, Steinway's Director of Concert Services. As Horowitz worked that note, and it wouldn't respond properly, David said, "Let's call Franz. He's just across the street in the Midtown Motor Inn. He can come over and fix that note."

And Horowitz said, "Oh, don't bother him. I'm sure he is running after the girls of Boston and having a good time."

Mr. Rubin got very serious, and said, "Oh, Mr. Horowitz, you don't know Franz. He would never do that. Franz is a wonderful Christian fellow who loves his family, and I bet he is reading his Bible right now. He reads his Bible all the time."

Well, Horowitz was stunned by this, and said to Mr. Rubin, "Call up Franz and ask him what he is doing."

Mr. Rubin called me, and I was indeed, at that very moment, sitting in my hotel room reading my Bible and making notes, because the following weekend I was to be teaching an adult Bible class in my church at home. So here comes the call, and David Rubin asks, "Franz, tell me what are you doing?"

And I said, "Well, I am reading my Bible and making notes for teaching my adult Bible class next week."

Rubin exclaimed, "I *told* Horowitz that! Can you come right over? Bring your tools and fix a note, please. Horowitz broke a note on this piano."

I took my tools and hurried over. Before I could even put my bag down and start work on the piano, Horowitz said to me, "Franz, tell me what is that you believe? What is that about your faith? Mr. Rubin told me you are a believer, and that you read your Bible all the time. Tell me about that."

I told Horowitz the story of how I came to know the Lord Jesus Christ personally—years and years ago—and how I am now the most happy person. (This story is told in chapter 11. It is the center of my whole life, as well as of this book—because for me Jesus is everything.)

Horowitz at that time really listened, and seemed greatly moved by my story. He said at the end, "Franz, that is some story." Then he said, "Here is my wife, she is Catholic. But Wanda, she believes nothing. She doesn't go to church." He then said, "I am supposed to be Jewish, but I have nothing whatsoever of faith." He paused and then went on, "Franz, I am really moved by your story. I ask you this: If I invite you—I only have a few friends, but all my friends never heard a story like this, I am sure—if I invite you to my home, would you tell this story to all my friends?"

I said, "Maestro, I would love to do that. I would love to do that."

Unfortunately, the invitation never came.

Yet I did have a few more opportunities to talk to Horowitz about salvation and eternal life. A few weeks before our last trip to Japan together, in the summer of 1986, we were doing some recordings in Studio A, the famous recording studio in the RCA building where many important artists recorded. One day during those sessions, Horowitz looked up at me from the piano and asked, "Franz, how long have you worked for me?"

I had no idea what was coming next, but I answered, "It must be over twenty years now that I have worked for you."

Then he said, "How come that you never invited me to dinner? I have never been to your home. You are still alive, your wife then must be a very good cook." He always had a tremendous spontaneous sense of humor. Then he said, "Why don't you invite me?"

I said, "Maestro, would you come to my home if I invite you? I'm your tuner, that's all."

He replied, "Sure, sure I come. If you invite me I come with Wanda."

Well, I got a little bit frightened after that. I went home and said to Elisabeth, "Dear, Horowitz is inviting himself for dinner at our house." And she got a little bit afraid too, and said, "Well, we know he is so fussy with his eating. We never will be able to give him a meal which he likes."

"Oh well," she went on, "it's best not to mention it. He probably will forget all about it. He will forget he asked you."

But he *didn't* forget it! The next recording session, which was in a few days, here I come to the studio, and when he comes in the first thing he says is, "Franz, what about Saturday? We come Saturday to your home—is that all right?"

And so . . . he came.

Knowing that he only eats fish or chicken, we decided on a chicken dinner for him, and Elisabeth decided on her favorite recipe for chicken.

On the Thursday before he was to come on Saturday, Juliana called from the Horowitz home and said, "Please understand, Elisabeth, Maestro just gave me the menu of what he would like to eat when he comes on Saturday"!

So here was the menu: He wanted Dover sole—gray Dover sole, broiled; he wanted a little bit of pasta first; he didn't want any wine but he wanted Evian water; he wanted only lemon and oil on his salad of lettuce; and for dessert he wanted baked apple with a little honey on the side.

And, he wanted all our children to be there! So I invited Peter and his wife Elizabeth, Michael and his wife Donna. Our Ellen was in college then so she couldn't make it.

We prayed quite a bit about Horowitz coming for dinner, and about all the unusual arrangements. I had to drive to New York to pick him up. He didn't want to come in a limousine. "No, no," he said. "No, Franz—*you* pick us up." So I picked him and Wanda up on Ninety-fourth Street, and drove them to our house.

We had put our big German shepherd dog in the garage,

locking him up so that he wouldn't come near Horowitz. But as
I parked the car, Duke was barking like everything, jumping up
and looking through the window of the garage to see the company who was coming. Horowitz, loving dogs, immediately
went to the window and said, "Hi, doggie. Hi, doggie. Franz,
what a beautiful dog! You have to bring him in!"

I did that later, as Horowitz wanted to say hello to Duke. I
brought him in on a short leash, holding him. As Horowitz was
petting him, Duke growled a bit. Although he never did bite
anyone, I was afraid of that unusual little growl, so I held him
tightly, just in case.

Horowitz and Wanda had a marvelous time. They didn't want
to go home. It was between 12:30 and 1:00 A.M. when they
broke it up, and then I had to drive them all the way back to the
city (over an hour's drive). But the evening was a smashing
success!

Before dinner, as we sat down together I wanted to pray. I
said, "Maestro, may I pray? Because it is the custom in our
house to pray before we eat."

Horowitz turned to Wanda and said, "Wanda, didn't I tell you?
We go to Franz and he is going to pray."

Then he turned to me and said, "Go ahead . . . pray. You won't
hear any amen from me . . . but pray."

So I prayed. Not only did I thank the Lord for the food and
ask him to bless it, but I thanked him that the Horowitzes had
come to our house. And I said something like, "Lord, it is our
prayer that Maestro and Wanda Toscanini would become as
certain and happy in the faith as we are." Then I prayed for the
success of the concert tour in Japan. Well, Horowitz did not say
amen, and we left it alone. All evening he had a great time.

Horowitz brought a very fancy cake to us. He didn't touch it,
but it was large and everyone had a piece. A funny thing happened as we drove back to the city, showing Horowitz's humor.
As we came to a toll booth, he suddenly turned to me: "Listen,
are you every time paying two dollars for this?"

I said, "Oh yes."

So then Horowitz said, "Then today you paid eight dollars for me, going back and forth."

I said, "That is correct."

Horowitz nodded and said, "Then we are even. I brought the cake, and the cake cost twenty-eight dollars. So we are even."

While we were driving Horowitz exclaimed several times, "What a rich family, Wanda. This family is so rich and so happy, we have nothing of this . . . nothing of this." He repeated this several times; he was quite taken by the family atmosphere, meeting our children and having a good time with us all. As we drove down Fifth Avenue and turned into Ninety-fourth Street, his street, he said, "Wanda, what a beautiful family. How rich they are." And Wanda didn't say anything. Horowitz was sitting in the front beside me, and he said, "Oh, Wanda is not speaking." He waited then for an answer from Wanda, but still she did not speak. There was Wanda sitting in the back, and she was silently crying. Then Horowitz said to me, "Oh . . . Wanda is thinking about Sonia."

Sonia was their daughter, the only child they ever had. Sonia tragically died when she was thirty-six years old, in Italy. She died so suddenly and so young. Steinway sent me up to their home and I was supposed to try to talk to them and comfort them. Wanda had said, "Our Sonia was quite sick for months, and you know what . . . she didn't read anything else but the Bible for those months. The last few months of her life, she read nothing but that Bible which someone had given her."

My hope is that she died a believer.

It really amazed me how often the subject of death and dying came up when the Horowitzes were with me.

The story of the dinner at our house had a "continuation" a few weeks later in Japan. When we came to Japan, there was a special formal dinner given at the famous Imperial Hotel in Tokyo. A lot of people were there—the Japanese promoters of the concerts; Richard Probst, the Director of Concert Services, had come from New York Steinway; our Steinway dealer was there with his wife and mother; and some leading Japanese people—there must have been about twenty-five people there. Everyone was talking and having a good time. The drinks came first, and then many waiters coming to serve the food.

While the main course was being served, all of a sudden Horowitz cried out, "Silence! I want everybody to be quiet. Quiet, please." Then, when everybody was quiet, he turned to me and said, "Franz, I want you to pray with us as you did at your house. I want you to pray as beautifully as you prayed in your home, when I was there for dinner."

I felt overwhelmed. But I prayed. I don't remember just what I prayed, but I prayed. Within me, silently in my spirit, I praised God that something had struck in the heart of Horowitz when I had prayed at our dinner table.

There is an emptiness in the heart of any human being who does not have a relationship with his or her Creator. Anyone who does not have a relationship with the Creator, the heavenly Father, is missing something tremendous in life. No matter how much fame or money or success that person has, it cannot make up for what is lacking. The heart cries out for God, even if the person does not know what he or she is crying out for. I have seen this time and again.

I remember especially one time after a Horowitz concert in Boston. Elisabeth was with me, and Ellen, who was attending Gordon College nearby. After a truly magnificent concert we were all together in the dressing room of Seiji Ozawa, the conductor of the Boston Symphony. Horowitz was sitting on the corner of the couch, now utterly exhausted after that successful concert, while people were talking to him. Wanda Horowitz, Elisabeth, and Ellen were standing together . . . and Wanda looked us straight in our faces and said, "If this is what life is all about, I don't want it."

I said, "Mrs. Horowitz, there is something more to life than this."

"Oh," she said, "I know what you are going to say . . . I know, I know . . ." And she didn't want me to say anything else.

There are so many stories told about Wanda Horowitz, who is the daughter of Arturo Toscanini, the famous conductor. Many describe her as abrasive and difficult, with no love and under-

standing of Horowitz. That is definitely *not* that case. Elisabeth
and I really admire Wanda Horowitz for her straightforwardness.
In my opinion she was Horowitz's best critic. Whenever she was
unable to go to a concert, Horowitz was really lost without her.
He depended so much on her honest and straightforward judgment, even in matters such as where to put the piano. No
matter what we would tell him about how great the sound was,
he felt lost without Wanda there to reassure him.

One time during rehearsal in Carnegie Hall, Horowitz was
sitting on the stage and a few people were sitting down in the
audience—some of his friends, and of course Wanda. Horowitz
was extremely nervous that day, and I must say he did not play
very well. At one point he stopped and, looking down from the
piano into the audience he yelled, "Wanda, Wanda, how does it
sound?" But Wanda kept right on talking and would not pay
any attention to his calling. Finally Horowitz turned around and
spoke to himself, "I guess she is not talking to me today. I know,
I know . . . it is not too good." And then he went on playing.

That is exactly what it was: Wanda was not happy with his
playing, and Horowitz knew it, but she didn't want to say so in
front of all the people.

Just a few weeks before Horowitz died, he said to me, "Franz,
you know what? When I come downstairs I always read the
New York Times before I go to the piano and play." For many
years Juliana would lay out the sections of the *New York Times*
on the couch, ready for Horowitz to read in the order he liked.
Horowitz said, "Franz, you know what? I always used to read
the *front* page of the *New York Times* first. But, I got away from
this. Do you know what I read first now? I turn to the obituar-
ies, and I read that first. And I'll tell you what: If I do not find
my name there, I'm so happy—I'm so happy!"

He did not realize that just a few weeks later, his own death
would make the *front* page of the *Times*! "VLADIMIR HOROWITZ,
86, PIANIST OF POWER AND DELICACY, IS DEAD." Yes, he made the
front page; and there was an entire page of history and pictures
of the high points of his career also, on an inside page.

Horowitz's music can be heard by each of us as we put the discs or records on. Yet the reality of the person, being absent from his or her body at death, is just as God spoke of in his Word to his people. It was Job who so very many years ago spoke the words which are sung in Handel's Messiah: "I know that my Redeemer lives, and that in the end he will stand upon the earth. And after my skin has been destroyed, yet in my flesh I will see God; I myself will see him with my own eyes, I and not another. How my heart yearns within me." That comes from Job 19:25-27.

Job, a very early book of the Bible, speaks of the assurance of a man who trusted God, who in the midst of terrible affliction yet had hope of one day seeing his Redeemer, the Messiah, who would come so very many centuries later, and yet whom Job trusted as the One who could give eternal life—could give that which Malcolm Forbes said he wanted to have—a healthy body, a resurrected body that will last for not just a measured length of years, but forever. What glorious music Handel wrote for these lasting words.

2 Rubinstein

My work with Artur Rubinstein was not nearly as extensive as my work with Vladimir Horowitz. Rubinstein did not normally take one particular piano with him on his tours. He would use the pianos—and the piano tuners—available at each location. When he played in major cities, however, he would usually take a piano from our Concert Department at Steinway in New York, and I would go along.

Rubinstein was an entirely different pianist than Horowitz. Rubinstein never had the technique that Horowitz had on the piano, but he communicated music in a marvelous way. You could lean back and really enjoy the music as he played, while in a Horowitz concert the atmosphere was electrifying, and you would sit on the edge of the chair, just fascinated with what would come out of the piano.

The unquestioned genius of Vladimir Horowitz notwithstanding, I could never mention Rubinstein's name to him. When I first began working with Horowitz, the people at Steinway warned me, "When you are with Horowitz, never mention the name of Rubinstein." I could talk to Horowitz about other pianists, but always of course I had to tell him that he was the greatest.

Rubinstein also chose and played on quite a different type of piano than Horowitz. As I have pointed out, each Steinway is individual and feels different, and this is a great blessing for pianists, who are also different both physically and musically. In terms of spielart, Rubinstein needed an action which had more resistance than a Horowitz action. He liked to get into the keys and to feel that resistance. Rubinstein would never have been

able to handle a Horowitz action. He also liked a rich, deep
tone, a dark tone which some of the Steinways are known for.

When Rubinstein would return from Europe each year, he
would look for a different piano immediately. No matter how
much he might have liked the piano from the previous season,
no matter how fine his concerts had been that previous season,
he always chose a new piano each year for his important concerts. And he always knew exactly what he was looking for in
his new piano. You didn't have to help him choose one. He
recognized right away which one would be right for him.

Many artists, even though they can't really afford the luxury of
such a choice, will start getting nervous about which piano they
should play long before a concert, and will come to our Concert
Department and try out one piano after another. There have
even been artists who have ended up with two pianos on stage!
And that can be very expensive, for although Steinway does not
charge well-known artists a rental fee, they do have to pay for
the tuning and the round-trip shipping.

Rubinstein never suffered from such indecision. One year
when he came in to make a selection, I had lined up four or five
pianos I thought he'd like. He sat down at the first piano and
immediately fell in love with it. He turned and said to me, "Oh,
that is so beautiful. This one I take." Then he said, "Franz,
where do we go first?"

And I replied, "Maestro, you go to Washington first this time,
and then you go to Philadelphia." But I added, "Maestro, I have
more pianos for you to look at . . . right here."

He didn't even look at them. He said, "Either I have a relationship with an instrument immediately, or I don't have that
relationship. The instrument and I have to be one, and I have to
be able to express myself on it. I must be able to let go of myself
and get lost in creating the music . . . or . . . I *don't* have that
relationship and I look for a different instrument."

He didn't even touch any of the other pianos I had set out for
him.

People really loved Artur Rubinstein, because he loved people.
Whenever people sought his autograph, on the street or on a

plane or train, he would always stop and chat with them.

With Horowitz it was quite different. Horowitz was extremely shy and afraid of people he didn't know. Once as Horowitz walked the few steps from the Bellevue Hotel in Philadelphia to the Academy of Music, with a whole bunch of us around him (Horowitz was always surrounded by friends), a person tried to stop him, saying, "Maestro it is so good to see you. I am coming to your concert tonight." Horowitz very abruptly turned to walk around the man, saying only, "Good for you."

Not Rubinstein. He always had time for people. And he would really talk with them.

Rubinstein was also very easy to work for. He was extremely appreciative of whatever you did for him. He always thanked you. Horowitz could blow up if the piano was not in the right position, but not Rubinstein.

The marked contrast in these two men can be illustrated by an occasion some fifteen years ago, when they played concerts just one week apart in Washington, D.C. This was before the Kennedy Center was built. At that time all the important concerts took place in Constitution Hall. One Sunday there was a concert with Horowitz, and the following Sunday one with Rubinstein.

I had promised my oldest son, Peter, who was about twelve years old at the time, that I would take him with me to Washington to the Horowitz concert. I told him I would also take him to some of the museums, including of course the Smithsonian. Peter was very eager to see Washington and I was looking forward to being able to show him some of the sights. I told David Rubin, our Director of Concert Services at that time, "Mr. Rubin, I'm taking Peter along with me to Washington this time."

"Oh . . ." he said, "Franz, don't do that. You know how Horowitz hates children. Don't take him. Don't let him come near Horowitz."

Well, I had promised Peter, and I was not going to change my mind about this. I wouldn't break a promise like that. But before the rehearsal in Constitution Hall, I said to my son,

"Peter, go way up . . . all the way up in the last row there." I
went on to explain, "Peter, you sit down up there, and don't you
move when Horowitz starts walking in. He is very funny about
children. He doesn't want to see you."

Soon Horowitz and his entourage walked on stage. Now, at
that time Horowitz had a poodle, a very nervous dog. We called
him a "piano dog" because he had only three legs—that is, his
fourth leg was much shorter than the others. The story goes that
one day in New Milford, Connecticut, when the Horowitzes
were staying in their country home, Mrs. Horowitz accidentally
ran over the dog with the car. So he lost a couple of inches of
that fourth leg. As Horowitz walked on stage with his
entourage, the dog followed, and started to sniff around and
bark . . . then he left the stage and started to run, and ran
straight up and back . . . all the way (you can imagine this)
straight to the place where Peter was sitting! Then he began
barking at Peter like crazy.

Horowitz, sitting at the piano now, and hearing the commotion of the dog's barking and running, turned around and peered
into the darkened hall. "Who is *that*?" he asked sharply. "Who
is that up there?"

Now, Horowitz was funny about anybody he did not know
being at a rehearsal. We always had to make sure that there was
no one in the hall who did not officially belong there. So he was
peering up into the darkness, and of course Peter was sitting
there, and Horowitz was indignantly asking, "Who is that?"

So I said, "Maestro, that is my son Peter. I brought him to
Washington with me, as I had promised him I would."

He simply said, "Oh, I see," and turned back to face his piano.

The next weekend as I came to Washington once again, I
brought my younger son, Michael. I had made the same promise
to him, and this was to be *his* weekend. This time it was Artur
Rubinstein's concert. At the rehearsal on Saturday I introduced
Michael to Artur Rubinstein. Of course Michael was excited, but
Artur Rubinstein was even more excited. He said, "Michael,
come here!" And he took him over to the piano and sat down
with him on his lap. "Michael," he said, "look at it—look at the

hall! Tomorrow all those seats will be filled with people." And he said, "There, maybe, in one of those first rows, there will be a beautiful girl sitting. And I will play just for that young girl, as if she were the only one. I will have her in my mind as I play."

I don't know how much Michael understood of that story, but Rubinstein then said, "Michael, do you play the piano?"

Michael responded, "Yes, I play classic."

Rubinstein said, "What do you play, then?"

Michael said, "Oh, I know the 'Wild Horseman' by Schumann—by heart."

Rubinstein asked, "Then would you play for me?"

Michael was so at ease with this man that he said quickly, "Sure!" And he played a few bars.

"Oh, Michael," Rubinstein exclaimed, "that is very nice!"

That was the difference between the personalities of Rubinstein and Horowitz.

Let me tell you about meeting Artur Rubinstein for the first time. It was at Woolsey Hall at Yale University in New Haven, during the 1963-64 concert season. Rubinstein was already a very big name in Europe, especially in Germany. Although I had done concert work in Germany before coming to the United States, I had never been privileged to work with Rubinstein. So I was excited to finally be meeting him.

Rubinstein, like most of the well-known pianists I have worked with, was Jewish, and had lost many of his relatives in the Holocaust. I knew about that, and wondered how he would accept me as a German. I had read an article where he was quoted as saying, "There are two places in the world where I never will perform. One is in the Himalayas, because that would be too high to bring the piano; the other is in Germany, because Germany is too low for me." He also had said he would never speak German again, although he could speak German fluently.

So while I was excited about working for Rubinstein, I was also a bit apprehensive. I simply prayed, "Lord, bless me, and make me a blessing for him too."

After tuning the piano for Rubinstein that first time, I was introduced to him backstage. He was very kind and gracious to me, although of course as he heard my accent he must have immediately noticed that I was German. Right away I said to him, "Maestro, I am so excited to be working with you. I come from Germany. I have worked with Steinway over there, but now I am excited to be here to work for you."

He responded, "Young man, did you clean the keys for me?" And I said, "Maestro, of course I did, I always clean the keys after I tune the piano. I always wipe the keys clean."

"Oh," he said, "somebody should have told you. *No* tuner ever cleans the keys for me. Of course you didn't know. You couldn't know that. We should have told you."

By now he was becoming furious; he said, "Well, I cannot perform tonight. Anyone cleaning my keys, makes my keys so slippery . . . I cannot play."

That was quite a situation! The concert was about to start. The orchestra was all in place. People were expectant. The program had prepared them to be ready for Beethoven's "Emperor Concerto." You can imagine that we didn't know what to do. What *could* we do? There is the soloist standing there firmly saying, "I cannot play!"

A few people were standing there backstage and one man said, "Maestro, I have a remedy." We all looked at this man and he continued, "I have seen this done, and artists have used this before . . . and really it works very well."

What was he going to say? We all wondered.

"Let Franz go out there on the stage with a hair spray can . . . yes, it really works! And let him spray the piano keys with hair spray. Then we will wait a few minutes until the keys dry and are a bit sticky. You will see, Maestro, you will do fine. This makes the keys 'grippy,' and you will love it."

Rubinstein thought it might be worth a try, so he said, "Go ahead."

From somewhere—I'll never know where—came a can of hair spray. I took it and walked out on that stage, into the lights, all dressed up in my dark suit. Of course the audience was all ready to hear the concert begin. The lights had been dimmed in the auditorium, and the stage lit up. The orchestra was sitting in readiness . . . and here comes this man with a spray can!

The people started clapping because at last somebody was walking out and they thought the concert was really going to begin. I didn't know what to do, except to keep on walking over to the piano . . . and then I began——pssssssss . . . pssssssssssss . . . the spray hissed out of the can and spread over the keys. Up and down, up and down I went, being sure that spray covered all the keys. Nothing slippery would be left when I got through . . . pssssssss . . . over all the keys. The people didn't know what to make of it. Some laughed, some clapped. I didn't know what to do . . . so I took a few bows, and then walked backstage.

We waited about ten minutes and then Rubinstein walked out . . . and the concert went on. Rubinstein loved that keyboard so much that I always had to carry a can of hair spray with me wherever we went! He wanted me to spray the keyboard with spray whether the keys were dirty or clean! It provided the kind of "grippy" feel that he liked.

Rubinstein was a wonderful gentleman to work for, and we eventually became friends. Although he said many times that he would never speak German again, occasionally when I was alone with him in his dressing room, he would slip into German and talk quite a time in German with me. I was very deeply touched by this. And many times I prayed for him. "Lord," I would pray, "please open the door that I may share with Rubinstein what I believe. As you know, Lord, I have a deep love for the Jewish people, especially as a German Christian, because of what happened to them in Germany."

I have always had a deep love for the Jewish people, even long before I came to the United States. In fact that probably was one of the deciding factors in our coming to the States. We never could understand the hate in Germany for Jewish people. When we left in 1960, that hatred still had deep roots among some Germans. Christians who really know the Bible know how important the Jewish nation is to the history of Christianity. They remember that Jesus himself said, "Salvation is of the Jews."

I prayed much for Rubinstein, and one day I thought I would talk to him about the gospel. I don't remember what I said, but after just a few sentences he cut me off and said, "Don't worry about me. When I get to heaven, I have no problem. I am Jewish, and if Moses is there at the gate, he will let me in. I have no problem. You know my wife is Catholic—maybe it is St. Peter who is at the gate . . . so *he* will let me in. And I have a son-in-law who is an Episcopalian minister—so how can I lose!"

That was in his dressing room in Avery Fisher Hall, and there were several people standing around, having a good time, and they all laughed at his response. Of course that shut me off, and I did not talk to him any more at that time.

One day in Steinway Hall Rubinstein said to me, "Young man, where do we come from? Why are we here? Where do we go?"

"Maestro," I said, "these are all questions which are answered in the Bible, which is the Word of God, and which was inspired by the Spirit of God."

"Inspired? Inspired?" he exclaimed. "Well, so are the letters of my mother. So don't tell me any more about the Bible being the Word of God. Forget it!"

Years later we were in his dressing room in Severance Hall in Cleveland. As I sat there alone with him, Rubinstein looked at a pile of letters addressed to him, lying on the table. There was a package there too. "Franz," he said, "do me a favor. Read some of that stuff. Read me some of those letters while I get ready." By that time his eyesight was beginning to fail.

So I started to read some of the letters. I will never forget this package with a book in it, and the accompanying letter a dear lady had written him. "Maestro," she said, "I am very concerned about some of the statements which you made and which have been publicized, saying that you are an agnostic, and that you don't really know about spiritual matters, or believe anything. Here is a book which will give you a lot of answers about spiritual things. I pray that you will read it. I know that you cannot read very well anymore, but would you ask your wife in some quiet hour to read you this book. May it give you many answers."

It was Francis Schaeffer's book, *The God Who Is There*.

Rubinstein turned to me and said, "Franz, some people are so beautiful. They are concerned about the deeper things of life. There aren't many such ones, but I get letters occasionally like this." He was very touched.

He continued, "Tell me, Franz, what is this book all about?"

"Well," I said, "I can't give you an outline, but I will read you some of the chapter headlines." He seemed really interested at the time. I only hope and pray that somebody did read this book to him.

There were so many stories going around about Rubinstein that were not accurate. Once I got excited because quite a few Christian publications stated that Rubinstein had said while he was in Israel that Jesus was the Jewish Messiah, and that he had made a decision for Jesus. I read that and was excited to believe it—but when Rubinstein came back to New York for the next concert season, I asked him about it and he said it was absolutely *not* true. He said, "For me, Jesus was the greatest Jew who ever lived. But . . . the Son of God? Forget it!"

One time as we were coming back from Europe Rubinstein said, "Franz, what do you think? Should I maybe play once more in Germany? I know it would be a tremendous success. But not only that: It would be, I believe, a good sign that I do forgive, and that I love the German people. They are *not* all the same."

I replied, "Maestro, it would be so wonderful if you would do this. It would be a wonderful gesture and it would do a lot of good, and be a blessing to many people." Unfortunately he never got around to playing in Germany again, although he did play one of his last concerts in Amsterdam, where half of the audience was German.

I remember so well one of the last concerts Rubinstein played. It was in Cincinnati, and it really shows you what kind of a person he was. I picked him up along with his manager at the airport, and right away he said, "Before going to the hotel, I really would like to see the piano and play a little bit."

So we drove to the hall. I had already been there in the

morning, and had prepared the piano and believed that it was in good shape. But as he played, he said, "Something is wrong with the piano. I don't know . . . it doesn't sound right. I don't feel comfortable."

So I said, "Maestro, I have all afternoon to work on the piano. I will check it all over and you will be fine." So I did spend some time going over the piano, but I couldn't find anything wrong with it. To me, it was just fine.

Then came the evening concert and he played a Haydn sonata. Then, before going into his second number, he stood up and came backstage—something he seldom did—and stepped up to me saying, "Franz, there is nothing wrong with that piano. I just didn't feel right. I do thank you so much. The piano is just fine."

It shows you what kind of a person he was, considering that explanation to me of such importance that he would leave the stage to come back and reassure me, before going on with the second number.

One time in Philadelphia, the organizers of a concert did for Artur Rubinstein something I have never seen anyone do for any other pianist. It was around the end of January, at the time of his birthday. He must have been eighty-six or eighty-seven at that time. While I was working backstage on the piano, getting it ready for the concert that evening, there were chefs working on a birthday cake for Rubinstein—a very unusual cake. They took an old piano which was backstage, and they plastered the whole piano with marzipan! Then they built a tremendous cake on top of the piano. The chefs were working all day on that amazing creation. On a board all covered with the sugary marzipan, they carefully wrote with chocolate letters, "HAPPY BIRTHDAY ARTUR RUBINSTEIN."

When Rubinstein finished the concert that evening, they brought him back on stage after tremendous applause . . . and as the back curtains opened, they rolled out the tremendous piano cake, to be cut at center stage. There were congratulatory speeches. And each person in the audience received a little paper box with a piece of cake in it. The whole affair just shows how much everyone loved Artur Rubinstein.

I only saw Rubinstein once more after that. It was after his ninetieth birthday. He was staying at the Drake Hotel in New York, and was in a wheel chair. As I came into his room he was so gracious to me. We chatted about many things. His hearing was not very good. I had to shout. He could not see very well either. Still, we enjoyed our visit. Once more I could tell him that I continued to pray for him, and that I wished him well. We talked about that unusual birthday party in Philadelphia. We talked about the many other tremendous times we had experienced together.

We remembered a very funny thing which had happened in Boston. Rubinstein's piano had arrived very late for a concert. It was the middle of winter, with the snow several feet high and a bitter cold temperature. It was almost time for the rehearsal, and here the piano had just arrived, having been on the truck in the ice cold, probably over night. When it finally arrived on stage and we opened it up, it was just like opening a freezer. Rubinstein exclaimed, "How can I play that piano? I can't play it this way."

I said, "I can't tune this piano in that condition." One should never, never tune an ice cold piano to begin with. A piano has to gradually get used to any change in temperature. If a piano is really in tune before it is transported, it will usually come back into tune in its new surroundings, no matter how cold the journey has been. But this must happen gradually.

So the question for us, there on the stage of Symphony Hall in Boston, was how to help the piano warm up as fast as possible, but not too fast. The picture of how we did this will stay with me forever: We sat, Rubinstein and I, with our behinds on the keyboard, diligently trying to warm up the piano with our body heat . . . talking meanwhile to each other as if we were on two chairs having tea!

As we sat there a photographer came to interview Rubinstein for some newspaper, and he took pictures of the two of us sitting there on the keyboard of that Steinway!

By the way, our method worked—it was a fine concert!

3 Gilels

One of the greatest Russian artists I have ever worked for was Emil Gilels. He made his American debut in 1955. Horowitz, Rubinstein, Rudolf Serkin, and Gilels were my inheritance from Bill Hupfer, my predecessor at Steinway. I tuned for Gilels and traveled with him to quite a few concerts. He was a marvelous pianist, known for his elegant and romantic approach, and I remember some of the outstanding concerts in which we were involved together. Since he spoke little English, and very good German, we talked quite a bit in German and became good friends. He recorded with the Cleveland Orchestra under the direction of George Szell; he recorded all five Beethoven concertos in one year, and they were all outstanding recordings.

Gilels asked me several times to drive him to concerts in my own car, and I gladly did. When Steinway heard about my driving him, they were nervous about it. "Franz," they said, "you know all Russia is behind him, and if ever something should happen, you could be in deep, deep trouble." Nevertheless, because we were good friends, I continued to drive him. Of course there was always another gentleman with us—Gilels's "interpreter." He was from the Russian Embassy, and there was no doubt in my mind that he came along mainly to see that Gilels did not "get lost."

Emil Gilels was the first Russian I was ever privileged to give a Bible to. (After that initial opportunity, I believe that every artist I have worked for has received a Bible from me.) While he was here one year Emil said to me, "Franz, I am so homesick for Russia. I can't wait to get home to our little apartment on Gorky Street there in Moscow."

Although he had his wife with him, he didn't like America and always looked forward to the return trip to Russia. Of course they guarded him closely and he didn't see anything except the hotel room, and all hotel rooms are more or less the same.

"I play my concerts on the stage," he said, "and I don't meet people."

Somehow there was a still, small voice inside me saying, *Why don't you give him a Bible?* I came home that evening and told Elisabeth what had happened and how I felt about it. She said, "Well, why don't we give him a Bible. No one can buy a Bible in Russia."

So I went to the American Bible Society in New York and bought a Russian Bible. As it was right before Christmas, we decided we would give it as a Christmas present, and Elisabeth gift-wrapped it very nicely. I took it with me to the next rehearsal, at Carnegie Hall, and had it with me in my bag on the stage. There were always people around Gilels, so I patiently waited for an opening to give it to him.

Finally my opportunity came. Gilels's interpreter was called to the phone and got into a lengthy conversation. So I took the gift-wrapped Bible to the piano where Gilels was practicing and said, "Maestro, we have Christmas coming soon, and at that time we give presents to each other. Here is a present for you from Elisabeth and me."

Immediately he asked, "Franz, what is it?"

"Maestro," I said, "it is something you cannot get in Russia."

Very quickly he took it and put it away between his music in his attaché case. I was nervous about this, because the concert was to be that evening; he would be taking his music out of that case, and I did not know how he would react to having received a Bible.

Gilels played his concert that night, as always with a tremendous success, and the next morning I was working at Steinway when at 9 o'clock he called. "Franz! Franz!" he said, "what have you done?"

"Uh, oh" I thought, "What is coming now?"

Then he went on: "Franz, what have you done? You have

given us a Bible. Do you know what? We have never seen a
Bible in our lives. And I've always wanted to have one. And
now you gave me one. You know what? After the concert we
sat together on the couch, my wife and I, and we read, and we
read, and we read. You know right now my wife is sitting here
with me, and she is reading now—reading that Bible!"

Needless to say I was very excited. I prayed for Emil Gilels
and his wife as they went back to Russia with the Bible.

Then the next year Gilels came to America again. Elisabeth
said during that time, "Franz, since he was so open when you
gave him the Bible, why don't you invite them to our house."

I did invite them to our house, but he said, "Oh, Franz, thank
you very much; we would love to come, but we do not have the
time this year. But, when we come next year we will come to
your house."

All that year we prayed for him. When he returned the next
year, we were on the stage in Washington, D.C., in Constitution
Hall, and after the rehearsal we were sitting together relaxing,
when I said to him, "Maestro, remember that you promised me
you would come to our house with your wife . . . what about it?
Wouldn't you like to come sometime when it is convenient for
you?"

He got so excited and said, "Franz, let's see." Taking out his
book, he went through the schedule of his concert dates.
"Franz," he said, "There is only one Sunday when I am free
before we go back to Russia, and that is November 2nd." Then
he said, "We come November 2nd . . . but how do we do that?"

"We live out on Long Island," I said.

"Well," said Emil, "you come and pick us up—pick us up
early so that we can stay the whole day. Come about nine
o'clock, then we can have a full day in your home."

"Fine," I said, "then I will be at Essex House to pick you up at
nine o'clock on November 2nd."

Then as soon as I said it, I thought, *That is Sunday. I don't
want to skip church. How do we do that?* So I turned to Emil and
said, "Maestro, you know that is a Sunday, and we go to church
on Sundays."

Quickly he replied, "Well, Franz, we go with you. We have never been to church. We would love for you to take us there, to church."

I was so happy that this could happen. The church we belonged to at that time was extremely active, and was always filled to capacity. We always had to bring chairs into the aisles. There were people everywhere; even the altar area was full of people. There was a kind of little revival going on. So I called the pastor. "Pastor," I said, "my artist I work for from Russia has never been in a Christian church, and he wants to come to church with us on November 2nd. Please be so kind to have some seats reserved."

The pastor was quite excited and told me what he would be preaching on that Sunday.

Then I bought a couple of Russian New Testaments, and found the portions of Scripture which the pastor would be preaching on. I underlined these in the Russian New Testament so that it would be prepared for them to follow. When we got to the church, there were seats reserved for Emil Gilels and his wife, and Elisabeth and me. As soon as the pastor started preaching, I opened the Russian New Testaments and gave them each one and told them the pastor would preach on this. It was a very interesting situation. As the pastor preached in English, I would interpret in German for Emil, and he would turn to his wife and translate it into Russian. So there was quite a commotion in our pew during that whole service. And I could tell that Emil enjoyed being there.

When we arrived at our home, Emil exclaimed, "Franz, this is a beautiful house. How many families live here?"

I replied, "How many families? Why, it is only mine." (I should point out that we have just a nice, modest, one-family home—nothing elaborate.)

Gilels just couldn't get over it! He couldn't get over the fact that a piano tuner and his family could live in a whole house by themselves. He said, "This would be impossible in Russia! You know I live on Gorky Street in Moscow, but I have a very tiny apartment. It is just two-and-a-half rooms for my wife and me and my daughter. My daughter has a tiny baby now, so we live in a very crowded apartment."

We had a great time together that day. He was very relaxed, and played the piano for us. As we sat down together for dinner we prayed before eating, and I remember he and his wife were greatly moved. She made the sign of the cross as we finished praying. I was absolutely sure that she had some Christian background. We were really encouraged that day.

They went back to Russia after that, and I remember when they came the next year for his concerts, the first thing he said to me was, "Franz, that Bible is such a tremendous blessing. But, let me ask you a question: You see, I am sharing that Bible with some of my friends; would it be possible if you would get me some more Bibles?"

"Well," I said, "How many friends do you have? How many Bibles do you need?"

"Do you think it would be possible to get eight Bibles?" he asked.

Of course I gladly got eight Bibles in Russian for him to take back to his friends in Russia.

Unfortunately, Emil Gilels did not return to the United States again. After the Afghanistan war began, the cultural exchange stopped and he never returned. He died in 1985. When I came to Russia in 1986 with Horowitz, I met with his widow. She came to the Horowitz concert in Moscow, and she was extremely happy to see me again and have a little time together.

4 Cliburn

The name Van Cliburn has always been associated with concerts of great excitement. I was not Van Cliburn's exclusive tuner, but the concerts at which I tuned for him were always outstanding experiences. I was involved with the preparation of Van Cliburn's piano for the September 1989 gala opening concert of the Morton Myerson Performing Arts Center in Dallas, Texas.

For that event Van Cliburn played Tchaikovsky's Piano Concerto No. 1, with the Dallas Symphony Orchestra. In reporting the performance, the newspapers spoke of Van Cliburn as a "superstar." This he certainly is. In spite of all the criticism he has received over the years, especially from fellow musicians (much of it, I suspect, motivated by jealousy), he deserves this praise.

Just before I went to Dallas to tune for this special concert, I saw Horowitz. A strange thing happened during that encounter. Horowitz said, "I hear you are going to Dallas to tune for Van Cliburn. I tell you what, Franz: This young man [this was 1989, when Van Cliburn fifty!] has double the sound that anyone else has."

It was unusual for Horowitz to compliment a fellow performer like that, so I interpreted it as special praise.

Whenever Van Cliburn played, it was a tremendous event. I remember some outstanding concerts, especially those he played with the Moscow Symphony. They loved him in Moscow. During my first visit to Russia with Horowitz, I was asked time and time again, in both Moscow and Leningrad, "When is Van Cliburn coming back?"

Although I did not hear Van Cliburn in Russia, I do remember the outstanding concerts in both New York and Washington,

D.C., when he played with the Moscow Symphony, with Kondrashin conducting. However what I want to talk about in more detail are two or three especially remarkable events connected with Van Cliburn.

One of those was when he was going to perform during the summit meeting between President Reagan and Mikhail Gorbachev on December 8, 1987. At that time Van Cliburn had not played in public for about nine years. One day when I was in the Steinway basement, I got a phone call from Van Cliburn. Now, during all the years that Van was not playing publicly, I had been very concerned about him. I was frequently in his home, talked over the phone from time to time, met him at various times. He had come to Steinway several times to purchase pianos. Through those years, we had become friends.

Several times I had encouraged him to play publicly again. His reply was always, "Franz, I will come back, but not at the moment." Then suddenly comes this phone call, just two weeks before that summit meeting. It was Van Cliburn saying, "Franz, are you alone? I want to talk to you alone."

I said, "Nobody else is here, Van."

He then said, "Franz, I know you are a man of prayer. I have just been asked if I would play. That is, I have been asked to give a concert in the White House when Gorbachev comes for the summit meeting. Please don't talk to anyone about it, not even to your wife, but I want you to make it a real matter of prayer. Please pray about it now, as I must make my decision by tomorrow. Don't talk to anyone about it, just pray!"

I immediately prayed with him that the Lord would help him make the right decision. Then I said, "Van, I know you are practicing, and that you are in good shape. Why don't you do it?"

He said, "Franz, I already have a program of what I would play, but please don't talk about it; just pray, and then tomorrow I will make my decision."

Of course I prayed for him, and the next day he did decide to go to the White House. This was very exciting in many ways. I now needed to be in the White House for a couple of days preparing things. Van's favorite piano was coming from Dallas; then there was another piano which I thought would be excellent for him, so I prepared it at our Steinway dealership in Washington so that he could try it and then make his choice before the concert. Of course I had to tune and voice both pianos, as the choice would be his. In the end he decided on his own piano which had come from Dallas.

That performance was an extraordinary and rare occasion, combining many unexpected things. First of all, I met Linda Faulkner, who was at that time the White House social secretary. She had read Edith Schaeffer's book, *Forever Music*, which has a chapter about my life and the work of the Steinway Concert Department technicians. She told me she had given the book to President Reagan, and that he was excited about reading it and then having me there to prepare the piano for Van Cliburn.

At one point in the preparations for the performance, we were rehearsing in the East Room and the door was closed. Only a few people were there—Linda Faulkner, Van Cliburn, and a few others, when all of a sudden a voice asked for prayer for the concert, and for the summit meeting, and for our country. It was Linda, and she continued, "Franz, why don't you pray for us?" With the door closed we bowed to pray, and the Spirit impressed me to pray for the real peace which one day will come on the face of the earth, which can only come through the Prince of Peace, who is our Lord Jesus Christ.

After that came the summit meeting itself, and the formal session that followed, with all the television crews arranging themselves in position, and the whole dining room full of activity. President Reagan made his speech, and then Gorbachev. I was able to take several pictures during that meeting, but one in particular I will always cherish. It was a photo of Gorbachev, taken as he ended his speech by saying, "God help us all." I remember thinking, *Gorbachev probably has a Christian background somewhere.* I knew in my spirit that he was absolutely sincere when he said, "God help us all." It was for me tremendously moving to hear the leader of the communist world making such a statement.

Then came the concert. There we all were, sitting in this formal room: Mikhail and Raisa Gorbachev; President and Mrs. Reagan; Eduard Shevardnadze; Vice President and Mrs. Bush. Billy and Ruth Graham were there. My seat was right at the tail end of the piano, so that Van Cliburn could see me. Later on he said, "Franz, you were such an encouragement. When I opened my eyes I always saw you sitting there, and I knew that you were praying, and this encouraged me very much."

It was a very formal concert. Cliburn played some Chopin—a light classical program, but no great excitement . . . until all of a sudden, when the formal program was all over, he decided on the spur of the moment to play, "Moscow Nights." Not only did he play it, but he remembered the Russian words and sang them to Gorbachev, leaning over toward him, and playing all the stanzas, all the verses.

The Russians just melted. It was quite a sight to see. They got excited as Van Cliburn said, "Sing along." As this all finished, they immediately jumped to their feet. Gorbachev embraced Van Cliburn, and it became quite an emotional moment. I was amazed that Van Cliburn, on the spur of the moment, remembered not only the music but all the words of that Russian song. You see a tremendous talent here, doing a spontaneous thing like that at such a moment. It was truly a touching and impressive experience.

There was another White House experience I would like to tell you about. This took place on Thursday, October 2, 1975. It was during the presidency of Gerald Ford, and Van Cliburn had been asked to give a concert in honor of the emperor and empress of Japan. I was to tune and prepare the piano, and expected after the rehearsal to fly on the shuttle back to New York. Then, quite unexpectedly, I got an invitation to attend the reception following the concert. I had tuned for White House concerts before, but had never been invited to a post-concert reception.

Although I was excited when the invitation came, I realized of course that it would be a "white tie affair." I had not come prepared to stay overnight, nor did I have a tuxedo. I mentioned this to Van Cliburn, and he said, "Franz, we will fix that!" He made a couple of telephone calls, and Van, his mother, and I all got into a limousine and went out to rent a tuxedo. We arrived at the tuxedo rental place shortly before 6:00 P.M. I got fitted, and Van then took me back to the Jefferson Hotel, a small hotel near the White House where I usually stay. I then called Elisabeth and told her I wouldn't be home till the next day.

It was time then to take a shower and dress, and put the tuxedo on, as I was going to be picked up at a precise time to be taken to the White House. As I was dressing I suddenly realized that, with all the things laid out, there was no white tie! Perhaps because we had been in such a hurry, the salesman or tailor had forgotten to put the white tie in with all the other things. I didn't know what to do. Here I was, preparing for my first formal reception at the White House, and I had no proper tie!

I called the White House, asking to talk to Mrs. Henderson, the social secretary. I told her of my dilemma and distress, and she said kindly, "Mr. Mohr, don't worry about it. Please just come without a tie. Because it is white on white, it won't be that noticeable."

Still I didn't feel right about it, and felt I must find a solution. I went down to the lobby and asked several guests if they had a white tie, but none of them did. I noticed that the waiters in the dining room wore black ties. I asked if any of them had a white tie, but none of them did either. As one of the diners in the dining room heard of my dilemma, he suggested, "Why don't you go across the street to the Hilton Hotel and maybe you will find something there."

So I crossed the street to the Hilton. Now, you should know by now that I always stop and pray for help in such situations. And I did so right there: "Lord, please show me what to do about this." As I looked around again, there in the drug store of the Hilton Hotel, I found a package of white men's handkerchiefs, and I got an idea. Looking around some more I found a sewing kit which said, "Greetings from Washington, D.C.," and added it to my purchases. I ran back across the street to the Jefferson and up to my room and as quickly as possible put together, from two handkerchiefs, what seemed to me a reasonable white tie, and then fastened it with the needle and thread to my collar!

As I went on dressing and looked in the mirror after finishing my invention, I realized that the tie was much too big. But it was too late now to make it smaller. I gazed in the mirror, wondering what to do. The limousine would arrive any minute now to pick me up and take me to the White House. I could only go on, wearing my unique tie!

I arrived at the White House and went to the library, where they had put a small piano for Van Cliburn to warm up on. He was in a frustrated state, as someone was supposed to have brought him the music for the Japanese national anthem, which he didn't know and had never seen.

Van Cliburn's manager, Harvey, then said, "Van, we will pray about this, that this piece of music arrives in time for you to learn it, and that there will be no problem."

At that very moment someone burst into the room bringing that piece of music!

Van Cliburn glanced at the music, then sat down at the piano and played it without even looking at it, except to check a few notes here and there. I don't know if it was out of fun or if he was really serious, but he then said to me, "Franz, I want you to sit right behind me, or in the second row at least, and if I get stuck as I'm playing the Japanese national anthem, you must bring me the music!" I can't tell you how very nervous I was about that responsibility!

After the dinner, before we went upstairs, everyone filed past the emperor and empress and the president and first lady, and each one was introduced to them before going to the East Room for the concert. Just before Van Cliburn and his helpers went upstairs, we went into the library and prayed together, asking that God would be honored through the concert, and that Van would play well (and wouldn't get stuck on the Japanese national anthem!). Then we too filed by the emperor and empress, and went to the concert. I had the music stuck under my arm, and got to sit in the second row, right behind the emperor and the president.

There I was in that spot, with people coming into the room, talking to each other, not all sitting down yet, when suddenly Van Cliburn said to me, "Franz, that is a very unusual tie you have on there. Where does that tie come from?"

So I told him how I had made that tie. Van Cliburn got so excited that he turned and told everyone, and people stopped their conversations. "Look at Franz's tie," he said, "he made that tie himself! Look!"

I have a photograph from that evening which I treasure very much. There is Van Cliburn at the big concert grand piano. You see the audience full of dignitaries, Kissinger and his wife and all those other impressive people, and there right in the second row I'm standing. Everyone was standing up for the Japanese national anthem, and there, between Betty Ford and Emperor Hirohito you see me, with my enormous white tie! I treasure the photo as a reminder of how God helped me in a difficult situation.

After the concert I was talking with President Ford and remember saying to him, "Mr. President, I am a Christian. I pray for you and for our country all the time."

He said, "Thank you so much, that really encourages me."

Later on, Van Cliburn's dear mother began talking about Russia. She told many unforgettable stories of when Van went there for the Tchaikovsky competition. Of course he won that competition and became famous and well-loved in Russia. He played there many times. This all took place in Khrushchev's time. One time they were invited to the Khrushchevs' home, and when they met Mr. Khrushchev, Mrs. Cliburn said to him, "You must know that we are Christians, and we go to church; and you should know that we pray for Russia all the time."

And at that Khrushchev got very quiet and said, "Would you like to go to church?"

Van Cliburn said, "We don't know where a church is."

"Well," said Khrushchev, "which church do you belong to?"

"Well, we live in the Fort Worth/Dallas area, and we go to the Baptist Church."

Khrushchev then said, "If you would like to go to church, I

can arrange it." So he did, and there is a famous picture of young Van Cliburn playing the organ at the Baptist Church in Moscow.

That day Khrushchev also told them, "You must know that I had a mother who always prayed."

That remark interested me very much. I have also heard it said that Gorbachev had a mother who prayed.

5 Gould

Of all the pianists I have served over the years, Canadian artist Glen Gould was by far the most eccentric. When I first arrived at Steinway in September 1962, Bill Hupfer had just fallen out of favor with Gould. Gould was a young man at the time, barely thirty years old. Hupfer had been at the Thirtieth Street Columbia Record Studios in New York City preparing Gould's piano for a recording session. As he finished tuning the instrument, Gould arrived. Everyone knew that Gould was very particular about his hands, so Hupfer did not greet him with a handshake. Instead, he rested his hand on the artist's shoulder and said, "Glad to see you. How are you, Glen?" Gould became furious when Hupfer touched him. He later claimed that Hupfer had injured his shoulder forcing him to cancel some concerts. Gould sued Steinway for three hundred thousand dollars.

The thought of taking on temperamental Glen Gould as my very first Steinway client made me a little nervous. It also made the people at Steinway nervous. Whenever I was sent to work on Gould's piano I was warned by the company—"Franz, please don't go near him. Don't touch him. Just tune!"

Gould was not only sensitive to touch, he was sensitive to the cold. He claimed that his circulation was poor. All year round, regardless of the temperature, he wore a slouch cap, a wool scarf, gloves, and a winter coat with the collar pulled up around his ears. He soaked his hands in hot water for at least twenty minutes before playing the piano. Occasionally he wore fingerless gloves when he played.

Though he never smoked or drank, Gould did use medication. The pockets of his coat bulged with pill bottles—remedies for everything. He always carried his music and other items in a black plastic garbage bag. He looked like a bum, but was very clean. After every recording session he would change his shirt and thoroughly wash his hands.

Glen Gould's style of playing the piano was unique. He sat low to the floor in a rickety, wooden folding chair with sawed-off, fourteen-inch-high legs. The chair seat was covered with a worn leather cushion and wrapped in a piece of threadbare upholstery. He bent forward as he played. Sometimes it looked as though his nose would touch the keyboard.

In 1957, on his first American concert tour, Gould's peculiar ways caused tension between him and Cleveland Orchestra conductor, George Szell. Hupfer was Gould's technician at the time. He had come early to prepare the piano for a rehearsal. As the time came for the rehearsal to begin, the orchestra got in place and Glen Gould sat like a monkey on his old chair in front of the Steinway. He put his black plastic garbage bag on the floor beside him. Then he took off his shoes and placed them soles up next to the bag. While Gould was warming up, Szell emerged from his dressing room. Szell was noted for being rather stiff and formal. Inspecting the orchestra from backstage, he noticed Gould. Infuriated by the artist's sloppy appearance, Szell announced, "I am not playing with that bum!" and stormed out of the concert hall. Some orchestra members and administrators talked with Szell and assured him that Gould would be better groomed by performance time. They convinced him to continue the rehearsal. By the end of the rehearsal Szell was impressed with the young musician. He was particularly impressed with his sensitive rendering of Beethoven's Third Concerto. Musically they understood each other very well. Backstage Szell admitted, "That bum can play the piano!" The account of this clash was talked about for years. Hupfer told me the story to prepare me for the kind of situations I would encounter on the road with Gould.

Gould's favorite piano was a CD 3 18 Steinway which had been built in 1945. For years he had searched for an ideal instrument and had tried many. When he tried the CD 3 18 he fell in love. He purchased it in 1960.

Like many of my clients, Gould was obsessive about the maintenance of his piano. I did my best to satisfy his demands. Over the years I earned his trust; he would not let anyone touch the piano but me. Regulating his Steinway was a challenge. He liked a very shallow touch—so shallow that it sometimes presented problems during performances or recording sessions. As a piano is played, the felt hammer head strikes the strings and then is steadied by the back-check. In Gould's case there was so little "after touch" that the hammer would sometimes dance between the strings and the back-check.

Although he was extremely popular—his concerts usually sold out wherever he played in the world—Gould didn't enjoy live performances. He disliked the pressure of trying to entertain a distant audience staring at him from the shadow of the concert hall. In 1964, at thirty-two years old, he gave up public recitals. His last concert was performed in Orchestra Hall, Chicago, on March 28 of that year. He once joked with me, "Horowitz withdrew from the public for thirteen years. I can wait twenty years."

Gould believed that public concerts would not exist someday. He envisioned that they'd be taken over by electronic media. This suited him. He loved the intimacy of studio recording. In the studio he could experiment. He could adjust his musical interpretation until it satisfied him. Unlike a public performance, he could correct the final product if he wished to.

It was fun to watch him during the recording sessions. Totally engrossed in the music, he would conduct himself whenever he had a free hand, and hum along. His humming can be heard on many of his recordings. Sometimes, unintentionally, his famous chair can be heard too. I tried to keep the chair repaired. The joints had come almost completely unglued and had to be held together with wire. The chair squeaked like crazy. Lubricating the joints with WD-40 helped some, but not enough. As Gould played, swaying back and forth, the chair squeaked loud enough to be heard on the recording. Many takes were ruined.

Gould had very strong opinions on how a piece should be interpreted. In the studio he was king. At least most of the time. During one particular session Gould was to play the piano accompaniment for the famous German lieder singer, Elisabeth Schwarzkopf. She was to sing a Schoenberg composition. Gould considered himself an expert on Schoenberg and proceeded to instruct Schwarzkopf on how to sing. He played with one hand and conducted the singer with the other. She went along with this for a little while but eventually became irritated by Gould's pushiness. Without warning, she abandoned the session, went into the control room, and announced that she was leaving. Gould did not appear a bit upset by this. He took a short break and then returned to record some piano solos, acting as though nothing had happened.

Many of the musicians I worked with, including Horowitz, were totally consumed by music. That is all that they could talk about. Not Gould. He had many other interests and he could focus on several activities at once. I can remember driving around town with him in his Lincoln Town car. (He loved Lincoln Town cars. That is all he would drive. He once said to me, "Franz, I found out that next year's model will be two inches shorter. So, you know what I did? I bought two Town cars this year.") The car was his office on wheels and was very messy. While driving he could carry on a conversation with me, dictate a letter to his secretary, and work on a writing project all at the same time.

Perhaps because of his constant creativity, Gould lived in a shell, protected from the outside world. He was difficult to relate to, always dead serious. Though he had several professional acquaintances and many fans, he had few friends. We eventually became close friends—as close as one can expect with a man like Glen Gould.

When I accompanied Horowitz or Rudolf Serkin to Toronto for a concert, Gould would want to spend time with me. He would pick me up at the airport and chauffeur me to my hotel. Though he never attended the concerts, he would meet me afterward and take me to his apartment located in the penthouse of a large office complex.

His apartment, like his car, was a mess. I had to tiptoe over piles of papers and other things lying on the floor to get to a chair. But it was a perfect home for Gould. He could play or listen to music all night after the offices were closed and not worry about disturbing anyone. A restaurant on the ground floor of the building stayed open till the early hours of the morning so, as was his custom, he could eat at 1 or 2 A.M. We spent many hours together listening to music, talking about many things, and eating dinner at odd hours.

It was rumored that Glen Gould was an atheist. In my judgment this was not so. He had a tremendous appreciation for Scripture, especially as expressed through Bach's cantatas and English medieval music. He once told me, "The Bible comes alive through music." Though he never joined a church, he said, "I'll have nothing to do with church. I don't fit in anywhere, but I am personally impressed with the lifestyle of the Mennonite Church and their doctrine. That is where I would belong—in a community like that." In 1973 he wrote a radio documentary about the Mennonites titled, "The Quiet in the Land."

Working for Gould was always an adventure. Sometimes he had trouble getting a room at the fancier hotels because of his slovenly appearance. This didn't bother him at all. As a matter of fact, he was proud to be mistaken for a bum.

One time when I was waiting for him to return to New York City from Toronto, I received a phone call. He said to me, "I have to cancel the session today. Go home. It will be tomorrow. I am here at Niagara Falls and they won't let me into the country. They won't let me through because of all the pills and stuff." He waited several hours for clearance by the border guards, who were concerned that he might be bringing illegal drugs into the country.

Some of the inconveniences we faced at the border were overcome when Gould moved his recording sessions from New York City to Toronto, in Eaton Hall. He loved the acoustics there. At one time Eaton's was a large department store—one of Toronto's landmarks. On the top floor of the Eaton Department Store was the famous hall. It was strange to go through a department store, walking past roped off store fronts, to get to a concert hall.

During the '70s the building was sold and converted to an apartment complex. While the remodeling was going on, we were often without heat or electricity. The hall was so cold at one recording session that several large propane heaters had to be set up in the aisles. Once the hall was heated, the heaters were turned off so that their noisy blast would not be picked up by the recording.

Though we no longer had to worry about getting Gould across the border, I had trouble bringing my tools from New York to Canada for recording sessions. The Canadians were very wary about my coming into the country to service the piano. I guess they feared that I was taking a job away from a Canadian piano technician. Sometimes I spent hours explaining to the border guards that I would only be working on Gould's Steinway and that he would not let any other technician tune it. As I explained they would comb their regulation books to determine whether I should be granted clearance. Inevitably, after a lengthy detainment I would be permitted to enter the country and care for Gould's Steinway.

The Steinway CD 3 18 is the piano heard on all of Gould's recordings but one. On the last recording made in 1982, Gould used a Yamaha. Many people have wondered why and Steinway has given me permission to explain.

After four decades of hard use, the CD 3 18, though slightly shabby, was still in great shape. I continually maintained the piano, replacing hammer shanks and other parts as necessary. But over time even the finest piano ages; the wood becomes brittle and the action of the instrument becomes worn. The day came when there was no way to repair Gould's piano other than to rebuild the action.

Since each Steinway is hand-crafted, no two Steinways are alike. Each instrument has its own personality which cannot be duplicated. When a piano is rebuilt, it is very difficult to reproduce the tone and the feel of the instrument that the artist is accustomed to. The piano key has to go down exactly with the same amount of grams as before. I know how to do it, but even when a piano is restored as precisely as possible to its original dimensions, it takes some time to break it in.

Horowitz always resisted having me rebuild his piano. He was very concerned that the feel of the piano would be altered. I promised him, "Maestro, it will feel exactly the same way you remember it." To ensure this, I made a chart of all the parts and the gram weight of each key. As I rebuilt that piano I duplicated the gram weight and the action as precisely as possible. I was prepared to do this for Gould.

Unfortunately, at the time I was swamped with commitments to other artists as well. Now we have eight concert technicians so the pressure is not quite as intense, but in the early '80s there were only two of us in the concert department. Due to my busy schedule Steinway asked me to let the factory do the rebuilding. "You tell them what they should do and then you follow up and finish the piano in the concert department." So I went over to the factory and explained to the rebuilders that it was very important to reproduce the action Gould wanted.

They worked for months on this piano—a whole summer. To my dismay, when I went to the factory and put my fingers on the piano, I knew that Gould would not be pleased. The action was much too heavy. I could adjust the voicing, but the feel of the piano could not be restored. I refused to try.

When Glen Gould and his friend Bob Silverman, the editor of *Piano Quarterly* magazine, came to the factory to inspect the piano, I did not want to be there. Gould put his hands on the rebuilt CD 3 18 and nearly broke into tears. "This is not my piano. What has happened to this piano? I cannot play it; I cannot use it." The piano, his friend for so many years, had become a stranger to him. The poor man was completely lost.

Gould was under contract with a recording company and had a pressing commitment to fulfill. In great desperation he searched for an acceptable substitute among the Steinway pianos, but could not find one. Horowitz's piano would have suited him, but Horowitz would have never let Gould use it.

Angry and frustrated with Steinway, Gould approached the Yamaha people. He found a Yamaha that needed some careful regulation but had an action similar to his CD 3 18. Alexander Ostrovsky, a well-known Yamaha technician and a very nice man, prepared the piano for Gould's final recording session. This was the only recording session to which I did not accompany him.

On October 4, 1982, at age fifty, Gould died of a stroke. At the time of his death, he had produced over eighty recordings. 20,000 papers and artifacts were collected from his personal belongings and donated to the National Library of Canada in Ottawa. Among those belongings is Gould's beloved CD 3 18—the piano that I had spent countless hours regulating so that Gould could make beautiful music. The battered old chair with the sawed-off legs is also there—the very one that I had tried so hard to silence.

6 With Horowitz in the Soviet Union

It was in April 1986, before the "Second Russian Revolution," and even before the days of *glasnost* and *perestroika*, that I went with Horowitz to Moscow and Leningrad. It was truly like going into another world. Edith has told you of the day she came to the Steinway basement and watched us load that famous piano, CD 314 503 for its flight to Moscow. There was great excitement that day, and photographers were recording all that was going on.

I arrived in Moscow at 6 P.M., and was met there by two people. There was Elena, representing the concert organizers, and Mark Kaplan, from the American Embassy. As we went through customs, one of the officials noticed the very large Bible I always carry with me. She asked me what it was. "It is my own Bible," I said. "I read it every day." Then she said, "Do you have any more Bibles on you?"

"Yes, I have this," I replied, and put my hand in my shirt pocket. I had a real small, thin, pocket New Testament with the Psalms in it. I had slipped it in at the last moment there in our Lynbrook home, when I saw it lying on the table. I had thought all of a sudden, "It might be a good thing to have that little Bible with me too." So I put it in my shirt pocket, where it fit perfectly.

When the lady asked me, "Do you have any more Bibles on you?" and I showed her that very little one, she took it and put it on the table next to the very big one and smiled. She didn't ask any more questions, and handed both Bibles back to me. I put the little Bible back in my shirt pocket, and my big Bible in my attache case, and was allowed to go.

Now I must say I also had eight Russian Bibles with me, which I had bought from the American Bible Society. I had prayed, "Lord, lead me to eight people I can make happy with a Bible," because at that time no one could buy them there. I had also prayed that these Bibles would get through the checkpoints. I was sure that the Lord had answered my prayer and had wonderfully made it possible for the Bibles to get through.

At this point I was shuffled into an office right there on the Russian side of the customs checkpoint. Mark was there, as was Elena, who now said she was my "interpreter, to take care of you." As I sat there, exhausted after the long journey, they discussed, in Russian, an apparent problem with my hotel reservation. *Why should there be a problem?* I wondered, *Everything was paid in advance.* I sat there growing more and more tired, becoming upset at not being able to get anywhere.

Finally Mark said, "I don't know what to do. I can let you make some phone calls and all that." He really tried to help me as much as he could.

I suddenly got up and went over to the man behind the desk and said, "You know, it is unbelievable here. We have had to pay in advance, like nowhere else on the face of this earth. We had to pay *everything* in advance: the moving of the Horowitz piano, the hotel rooms in Moscow, and the hotel rooms in Leningrad— every expense in advance. Now I arrive, and there is no hotel room!"

The man got angry and shouted, "The reason we are confused is because you kept on changing the date of your arrival."

Now that was the first big lie I heard in Russia: From the time we first began making our plans, the date that I would arrive to prepare the piano, and the number of days I would stay, had not changed.

Mark appeared again and said, "Well, Franz, here is what we're going to do. I will take you to the American Embassy.

One of the families that lives at the embassy has a free room, since they have a son away at boarding school in the United States. You can sleep there until all this has been cleared up."

The man behind the desk then said with an official air, "No, don't go to the embassy. We now have a room for you, a hotel room. It is outside of Moscow and that is where you will go." He didn't want me to go to the embassy.

But Mark quickly said, "No way will Mr. Mohr go there." Then he turned to me and said, "Franz, don't, please. That's foolish. Please don't go there. We'll take care of you." So they had a bit of a fight over what they would do with me. Mark won the fight, so I was finally driven in a car to the American Embassy. There I met Mr. and Mrs. Beal, who had offered their extra room. The next day it was still not clear as to where I was to stay, so I stayed a second day at the embassy.

My stay at the embassy was really very interesting. There was some kind of a party going on and I met a lot of different people. The Beals had about twenty-five people there, all Americans. I learned that they were all plumbers and electricians and other craftsmen, who had come from America to repair some things in the embassy. "We cannot trust any Russian workmen, so we have to use our own. They have just arrived, and we are having a party to welcome them."

It seemed strange to me, therefore, that all the young women serving refreshments at the party were Russians. If they feared that Russian workmen might be spies, why weren't they concerned about these waitresses?

Right after the party, Mark gave me an official piece of paper. "Read this when you are alone," he said, "but don't show it to anyone." Here's a sample of what I read on that paper:

SECURITY REMINDERS FOR VISITORS:
1. All telephone calls in the Soviet Union are monitored by the Soviets.
2. Assume that all rooms have electronic equipment to monitor all conversations.
3. Assume that all drivers understand English and are required to report all conversations.

4. Assume that all luggage and briefcases left in your room will be searched while you are absent.
5. Assume that all trash thrown in wastebaskets will be examined.
6. Do not leave any sensitive personal or official papers in non-secure rooms. You should work on classified papers only at the consulate general's. Remember that hotel rooms and other noncontrolled rooms are not secure for sensitive conversations.
7. Never use any names during a telephone call.

When I finally got to the hotel, I found it to be different from any hotel I had ever been in. On every floor there was an official to monitor all the people who came in and out of the elevators, or in and out of their rooms. This official wrote down the time you came in and the time you left! I had arranged to go out for breakfast the next day with our Concert Director from Steinway. As I stood knocking at his door at the appointed time, the official lady sitting at her desk said, "I would not disturb Mr. Probst."

I said, "Why not? We have arranged to go to breakfast together."

She then leaned over her book and said, "Mr. Probst came home at 2:38 last night. I would let him sleep."

That gave me a very strange feeling!

On the positive side, I have never had more beautiful hotel rooms to stay in than in this old world hotel in Moscow. I had three rooms with gracious furnishings, and a balcony view right across from the Kremlin. The room even included a concert grand piano! (I suspect it hadn't been tuned since the days of the czars!) I discovered that many of the hotel suites had pianos.

We had been told by our embassy people not to take a taxi at any time. "If you need a ride, we will always take you. Please call us if you need us and we will take care of you."

There were some exciting moments in Moscow, and some mysterious moments as well. For instance one morning—I believe it was a Saturday morning—there was a loud burst of band music, and I thought there must be a parade going past, maybe filling Red Square, so I quickly went to look out. But Red Square was empty. Then I saw groups of people coming together from different directions, gathering on the sidewalk. One person was taking their names—checking them in, so it seemed. They had shovels and other equipment. The march music was blasting out of loud speakers! Later on I found out that it was a "working day," for all the people in Moscow to report and go out to parks and other places, to beautify the city. Everybody had to take part in this, whoever they were, whether office workers or housewives. They had to climb into the backs of trucks which soon arrived, and be taken to the parks and other places where they were assigned to work. They had no choice about the matter.

Another day I had some time off and had nothing to do. I had met a number of people at that hotel, among them an American couple from Los Angeles who had come to Moscow for their honeymoon. I really couldn't understand why anyone would come to Moscow for a honeymoon in those pre-*glasnost* days, but there they were, really a nice couple. We had had breakfast together and during that meal they told me they had tickets for the evening for an ice hockey game. "Why don't you go with us?" they asked. "Germany and Poland are playing."

Actually it was the world championship games going on in Moscow at that time. So the Los Angeles man said, "Why don't you go downstairs to the office where we just got tickets. I'm sure you can get a ticket for this game too?"

So off I went to the tourist office and said, "I am free tonight and would like to have a ticket for the ice hockey game." The lady said, "Have you seen the circus while you are here?"

"No," I said, "I am not interested in seeing the Moscow Circus, but I would like to have a ticket for the ice hockey game."

She said, "You must see the circus first before you see any ice hockey game. The circus is so fantastic."

I argued with her and said, "Dear, I am really not interested in the Moscow Circus. Actually, I have seen the Moscow Circus in Madison Square Garden in New York City, when they were touring the United States. But I would like to have a ticket for tonight's ice hockey game."

Then she got kind of mad at me. She said, "I have *no* ticket for you. I am sorry, but come back in an hour."

So what could I do? But since I wanted very much to go to the ice hockey game, I went back an hour later and asked for my ticket. It was the same lady. She looked up and said, "I'm sorry. I have no ticket for you."

"But," I said, "you told me to come back in an hour, and you would have a ticket for me."

She then got very angry again and said, "I have told you everything I know." And she turned away.

Now, several people were sitting in the office, and one of them suddenly spoke to me in German, asking, "Are you German?"

"Yes," I said, "I am German born."

"Please come here."

So I went back into the office and without any problem another lady handed me a ticket and I paid for it. I thought it very strange that the lady who had refused me a ticket simply sat there and said nothing at all as I walked away with my ticket.

Horowitz was already famous in Russia when he left there in 1925. Knowing his popularity, the authorities deliberately played down his 1986 visit. There was little news coverage. Yet thousands were turned away, and there were many emotional scenes during and after the concerts. I remember especially one elderly lady who came backstage after the concert in Leningrad. With tears she told Horowitz that she had attended all his concerts before his 1925 departure. She even showed him a program he had autographed for her at one of those concerts!

As I mentioned before, when Horowitz heard that most of the students at the music conservatory couldn't come to his Moscow concert because it was sold out, and that most of the tickets had gone to the important people of Moscow, many to party bosses, he invited all the students to come to the rehearsal. And it was not a rehearsal in the usual sense, but a real concert, with no interruptions.

The scenes I saw that day were amazing. There were many students, all excited. But you can't imagine how quiet it was in that hall, with everyone so attentive. Some were even crying. Tears were rolling down their cheeks as they listened to Horowitz playing his program: the Mozart Sonata, the Scriabin Etude, the Scarlatti Sonatas and all that. He was simply tremendous.

Before the concert CBS did a three-minute interview with me. It was quite exciting as Charles Kuralt interviewed me about Moscow, Horowitz, and the concert. There was another event that was very special: a dinner party at the American ambassador's house, Spaso House, which was designed by an Italian architect and is as beautiful as our White House. At that party I saw Vladimir Viardo, a Russian pianist, and his wife, whom I had missed seeing as for thirteen years he had not been in New York. I also met Alexander Slobodianik, who also had not come to the United States for thirteen years. There was quite an excitement when I met these two Russian pianists and their wives at this dinner party. They were eager to talk to me.

Vladimir Viardo said to me, "Franz, Franz, you remember me, you must remember me. I am the one you gave a Bible to when I was in New York." Viardo, as you may know, won the Van Cliburn competition in Dallas in 1973. Afterwards he had played in New York. We became good friends during the time he was in New York. However it was soon after that, that the Afghanistan war commenced, and the Russian artists were forbidden to come to the United States anymore. To suddenly and unexpectedly meet Vladimir and Alexander again at that particular dinner party was a thrilling thing. At present they both live here in the United States, but that evening was an exciting reunion.

While we were in Moscow, Viardo invited us to his home, explaining how to get there. "Tomorrow, please come to our home and have dinner with us." The invitation was for me and Mr. Probst. As Viardo gave us directions to his home, he said, "Don't talk to each other as you walk. And at each corner, turn around and look to see that no one is following you. I am on the blacklist, you know. They don't want me to have any visitors from the West in my apartment. Please watch it. If you are conscious of anyone following you, then turn around and go back to the hotel. And don't talk to each other on the way back."

The directions he had given us were deliberately confusing. "When you get to my apartment, the door will be open. Don't knock. Please just come in."

So that is what we did. And we waited for him in his apartment for quite some time. The other pianist was supposed to come too, but he never showed up. However, we had a great time there. Viardo's dear wife had prepared us a wonderful dinner, and had little presents for us. It was really a warm welcome. We were amazed at the nice food we had, with fine vegetables. All the three weeks we were in Russia we did not see vegetables anywhere else! When we asked for vegetables in a restaurant the waiter had said, "It is not time for vegetables yet. It is only end of April." So I asked Viardo, "How do you have these beans?" He said, "Oh, there is the black market."

In 1989, during the days of *glasnost*, I saw Viardo at a party in New York, where he now lives. "Do you ever go back to your apartment in Moscow?" I asked. He said with a sigh, "Franz, we are really afraid to go back to Russia. We still have our apartment in Moscow, the one you were in, but we don't trust this whole situation. You know, we believe it can change within a few hours. The borders could close again and then we are trapped in Russia. This is something we do not want to have happen to us."

The dinner party at Spaso House was memorable for another reason. About a hundred guests were there in honor of Horowitz. There were many Russian diplomats and representatives from other embassies. While everybody was talking at their tables, suddenly Wanda Horowitz stood up at the head table where she was sitting and cried out, "Quiet, please. Everybody quiet. I want you to know, everyone here, that these people in the Soviet Union—they had nothing under the Czar, now they have even less!"

Then she sat down.

It was quiet for a time, then everyone began talking again. I never did know what triggered her statement, but Horowitz said to me later, "You know, Franz, I admire her for this. I am happy that she spoke up."

I wanted so much to take pictures inside the Kremlin, so every day I went to the gate. They have tourists walk over a bridge into the Kremlin, and every time I went to the gate they said the same thing: "You must leave your video here, then you can go in; and when you come out, we will give it back to you."

Then came my last day in Moscow. It was my last chance! Again they would not let me in with my video. I stood there for awhile when suddenly a busload of people came up and my colleague Richard Probst grabbed me by my arm and said, "Come, Franz. Come, we'll go," and together we went over the bridge, my video swinging from my shoulder, but nobody called us back!

So there we were, inside the Kremlin, and I took quite a few pictures. At another time in Moscow I was inside a church when suddenly there was a shouting voice and a hand seeming to come from nowhere, slapping itself over the lens of my camera. But my video was not taken away.

Of course many people have the recording, and some also have the video, of Horowitz playing in Moscow. It is a tremendous recording of a marvelous concert. It never ceases to amaze me how such a wonderful event, half-way around the world, can be brought to life in our homes on a video recording.

Going to Leningrad was also quite an experience. We did not want to fly to Leningrad, but to go by train, so that we could see the countryside by daylight. As we were trying to buy tickets we ran into trouble. There would have been no problem if we had asked for *night* train tickets, but they did not want us to go by daylight! However, through the embassy, with a lot of pulling of strings, we finally got tickets for the afternoon train.

Our Russian friends were with us. Elena from the concert

organizers, and Andre, a young Russian interpreter, to see that we "didn't get lost." Andre was an amazing young fellow. He was twenty-six years old, obviously well educated, and I think he spoke better English than I do. Yet I never felt totally comfortable around him! He went everywhere with me, even when I was shopping. If it was not Andre, it was Elena who went with me. I was never allowed to be alone.

The trip to Leningrad was really quite revealing. I'm sure that nothing had changed in that countryside from the time of the czars. We saw from the train windows old houses, old villages, crumbling walls, a kind of primitive farming unlike anything we see in Western Europe or America. We saw just a few fields here and there, but nothing growing, really looking like a wasteland. It had just rained and as we passed villages even the main streets were just full of ruts and stones. A look of neglect was everywhere.

As we rode along, at a time when everything was quiet, I took my New Testament from my shirt pocket and began reading a Psalm. Andre looked over at what I was doing and said, "What are you reading?"

I said, "This is my Bible."

Then he said, "You are not supposed to read the Bible."

I said, "Come on, Andre, I am American. You might not want Russian people to read the Bible, but I can read my Bible. You can't prevent me from doing that."

Then he said, "Of course I'm kidding. But, what are you reading in it?"

I said, "I am reading the Psalms."

He asked, "Can I see it?"

So I gave him my little Bible and said to him, "This is opened to the book of Psalms, which is part of the Bible. I am learning by heart Psalm 103: 'Bless the LORD, oh my soul, and all that is within me, bless his holy name.' You see I always learn a few verses, then close the book and repeat them. I know a number of Psalms by heart and it is a great blessing to me."

So he took that little New Testament and Psalms and began to read Psalm 103 where I had it open, and as he read the expression of his face changed. He looked as if he had been transported to a different world. As I saw this I prayed for him. After awhile he looked up and said, "Franz, this is very beautiful, very, very beautiful. I never saw such beautiful words."

Then I said, "Andre, listen, I read that Bible every day, but I have another Bible, my big Bible. So if you want me to, I will give this little Bible to you—if you promise that you will read it."

He was very happy to receive that little pocket Testament. He said, "You must know that my grandmother and also my mother, they both go to church. Of course not my father; men do not go to church in Russia. But my mother goes, and I know she prays, and so does my grandmother."

So he took my little Bible and read it. It was the last one I had except my own big one. I had given away eight Bibles by this time! It was amazing how the opportunities had arisen for me to give them.

For instance, I asked the Russian man who drove us for the American Embassy, "Do you have a Bible?"

"A Bible?" he exclaimed, "Nobody has a Bible in Russia. My mother, I will tell you, has some pages which somebody gave her from a Bible, and she reads those pages all the time."

"Well," I asked him, "would you like to have a Bible of your own?"

"Oh! Would I like to have a Bible of my own!" And so there went one of my Russian Bibles. The others I gave to various people, so when I was on that train to Leningrad, I had only the small Bible in my pocket and my big Bible left.

After a few days in Leningrad, it was very interesting that we each remarked the same thing: "The atmosphere here is different; it is not as tight as it was in Moscow." It seemed that people breathed a bit more freely.

Elena, the other interpreter, came to me after a few days in Leningrad, and took me aside. I felt she had something on her heart but was finding it difficult to say. Then she said, "Mr. Mohr, you gave a little Bible to my colleague Andre. Would you have a Bible for me too?"

"Well," I said, "I did have a few Bibles, but they are all gone.

The only Bible I have now is my own. But Elena, I tell you what, after we are finished here in Leningrad, a few days after the Horowitz concert is over, and we leave to go back home, I will be happy to give it to you.

She was so happy that I would give her my own Bible. You must know that in my Bible I have written all kinds of notes. I mark it up all the time. When I am reading the Bible or studying or listening to a sermon, suddenly I'll get a special blessing, or understand something profound, or see something I have not seen before; then I write a note in the margin beside that passage, to remind me when I read it another time. It was this Bible I finally gave to Elena.

I told Elena after that first day that I had not had an opportunity to meet any Christians in Moscow: Did she think I could meet some in Leningrad?

She said, "Let me find out." And she did find out! The secretary of the American Consul General also gave me a list of churches—Orthodox churches, and the Leningrad Baptist Church, where Billy Graham once preached. Elena came with the same information and on Sunday morning we went to this Russian Orthodox Church. We took a taxi and the driver drove us to two different churches, but nothing was going on. One was now a museum, and one was some kind of school. Several other big churches and cathedrals had nothing going on either.

Finally we handed him the address that Elena had brought, but he said he would not drive us to that one. We finally got somewhat loud about it, and he relented and drove us to that particular church. We had a hard time getting into the church, as it was filled wall to wall with people!

In the Russian Orthodox Church there are four different choirs which sing, one after the other, almost like stereo. The music echoes from corner to corner in the church as the choirs sing in different places, in the balcony. It was really very beautiful. I must say that I cried. I cried because not only did I see old folks but young folks there. There were soldiers in uniform with their girlfriends.

Elena and I visited the Leningrad Baptist Church on Saturday

April 26, 1986 after the Horowitz rehearsal. She arranged for a taxi driver to take us to the church, but he said he would only wait for a half-hour to drive us back. The whole thing would cost twenty-two rubles, which was very cheap.

As we drove in the taxi, Elena said she was so excited to go to that church for the first time, and she began to ask questions about atheism, about God, and some things she had seen. She talked about a painting in a Russian museum, a beautiful painting of a scene from the Bible, when the children of Israel had been very disobedient and were bitten by snakes. It was amazing how she had remembered all the details of that painting. I had seen it too, and I was able to tell her what it meant. So we were busily talking in the taxicab when we arrived at the church, and the service had already begun.

There were two people standing outside, greeting latecomers. One came immediately up to me, probably recognizing that I was a tourist because of the video camera over my shoulder, and spoke to me in Russian. Elena translated that he had asked, "Do you love Jesus?" I was so moved by that one question that I hugged him.

Another fellow spoke to me before we went in, and again Elena translated. He said, "You know, we are baptized believers."

I thought about that for some time, and finally realized he was saying that it costs something to be a believer in Russia, but that it costs even more to make that an open belief by being baptized. When we went in, the choir was singing. I do love the way Russians sing, and I'm glad I was able to bring that back with me on video. Elena was also deeply moved, and remarked that there were soldiers here too, with their girlfriends.

When the sermon started Elena interpreted it all for me. She really was excited by the youth choir in their white blouses looking fine and singing so well, and by the sermon by the visiting pastor from Finland. He preached in Finnish, and it was interpreted in Russian by the man standing next to him, and then into English by Elena sitting beside me. The sermon was about the woman at the well, from the fourth chapter of John's Gospel, where Jesus is telling her about her own life, and then telling her that he is the Messiah and that anyone who would believe in him would never thirst again. As Elena translated I could see that she was being touched by the content of that sermon. Suddenly the taxi driver who was sitting with us moved in his seat and said, "We have to leave now."

So off we went, and during the hour's drive back to the hotel Elena was asking non-stop questions about faith, Jesus, war, and atheism. Her heart and mind were bubbling over with unanswered questions. We were still in the middle of discussing so much when we got back to the hotel that I thought maybe we should have dinner together, to continue talking. Going to each of the four dining rooms, we found there were no places. I had a suite with three rooms and a balcony, as I had had in Moscow, so I said, "We could go up to my rooms and have a meal served there."

I ordered beef stroganoff, but she hardly ate anything, because of her continuing questions. And I was so busy answering her questions that I could hardly eat either! She wanted to know how I knew Jesus so intimately, and how I had had all my questions answered, and why I seemed so happy. So I told her my own story, which is also in this book, and she cried. We both hardly ate at all. Then I asked her at one point, "Elena, would you like to believe?"

And she said, "Oh, I have been so moved today. I have completely opened my heart to Jesus."

Then suddenly looking at her watch she exclaimed with fright, "I have to leave." And in one minute, leaving her food untouched, she was gone!

I had heard that Russian interpreters had to report to a higher command at a certain time, as to the things of that day. I couldn't believe that she had left with such fright and so suddenly, but I just prayed and committed her into the care of Jesus. After that I called room service and a waiter came to take everything away. He was very slow about gathering things up, and I thought that he must have something on his mind. All of a sudden he said in English, "Can I ask you a question?"

"Sure," I said.

"Do you have on you any religious literature?"

Once again I saw how hungry the Soviet people were for the Bible, for spiritual food. I sadly replied that I had given everything away, and my own Bible I had promised to Elena. The next day, before our departure, I remembered that I had an American Christian magazine, *Moody Monthly*, so I called him and gave that to him! I kept my word to Elena before leaving, so for the first time in many years I was without a Bible!

Horowitz had wanted to visit his hometown of Kiev, in the Ukraine. He had heard that his parents' home was still standing there. But he felt somehow uneasy about it, and decided not to go. On Monday, April 28, 1986, the day after the Leningrad concert, the Chernobyl nuclear disaster occurred. Chernobyl is just a few miles from Kiev. We were not informed of the tragedy until we were on the airplane bound for Finland.

The story of my video needs to be finished. Mr. Kassanov, who is back in the States now, was cultural attache at the consulate in both Moscow and Leningrad. He had accompanied us all the time, taking care of the Horowitz arrangements. He said as we went to the airport, "Franz, I can only help you so far, but I can't see any possibility of your getting out with that video going with you."

We had talked about this before in the dressing room at the concert, and Horowitz had also said, "Oh, Franz, you brought your video with you. I don't think you will get that out."

I had simply replied, "If the Lord wants me to get this video out, I will get it out." I confess that I was nervous about it, but I prayed, "Lord, if it pleases you and will honor your name, I will get it out; but I will not lie about it. If they take it away, fine; if not, I will use it."

So now here we were, ready to board the plane, and several Russian officers were opening the luggage of each passenger. First we had to give an account of our money, showing receipts for everything. Before I even opened my suitcase, the Russian man who was checking all my receipts became very impressed with a folding case I had, which has a writing pad, a neat little calculator, and all that sort of thing. It was given to me by Steinway in Hamburg and had my name in gold letters on the leather binding.

Inside the case were photographs, taken by a Russian photographer, from when I was tuning the Steinway on stage in Moscow. They were very poor quality, but the photographer had kindly given them to me and I was happy to have them. One of the pictures is of Horowitz sitting at the piano, with me standing beside him listening to his playing. In the photo, he was talking to me. Suddenly the young Russian checking me out said in fluent English, "Are you telling me that you are in the Horowitz party?"

I said, "Yes, I am his piano tuner. I tune for him for all his concerts. I have for twenty years. We just had the last concert here, and are now going back home."

The young man was excited, "I can't believe it! You must know I am a Horowitz fan. I have paid big money for his recordings. Now I have a half dozen Horowitz records in my home. I admire him so much." He was so taken by the fact that he had met Horowitz's piano tuner that he folded up my leather writing case, put it back in my case, and never even opened my suitcase with the videos in it! He asked no questions, simply saying with a smile, "You can go."

"Praise God," I said silently to the Lord. And that was my finale in Russia!

PART 2

The Piano

7 The Steinway

It has been my desire ever since I fell in love with the Steinway piano that, one day when I would write "my book," I would include a chapter on the Steinway, seen through the eyes of a musician and piano technician.

The story of the Steinway family and their pianos is fascinating. It is an American success story. My family and I, who like the Steinways came to America from Germany, can relate to their story in a special way.

For many decades of German history we looked at America as "Das Land der Unbegrenzten Moglichkeiten"—the land of the unlimited possibilities. I do not know in detail what motivated the Steinway family to come to America in 1850, but one thing is very clear: They felt limited and "boxed in" in their homeland, especially after the 1848 German revolution which had paralyzed all levels of commerce in the German states. As Heinrich Engelhardt Steinweg and his family read and heard about America, its free spirit and tremendous possibilities, the desire grew to go there.

Beside all this one of his sons, Karl, was in trouble politically after the 1848 revolution. The family sent Karl to America in 1848, to check out working conditions and the prospects for a manufacturing business there. At that time the elder Steinweg had twenty-five years' experience in piano building. Karl's enthusiastic letters home made it easier to make that otherwise not-so-easy decision—to leave the homeland and sail to America on June 29, 1850.

Making the voyage were Heinrich Engelhardt Steinweg, his wife Juliane, and five of his seven children (Doretta, Heinrich Jr., Wilhelmina, Wilhelm, and Albrecht). His oldest son, C. F.

Theodore decided to stay in Seesen, Germany, and continue
tuning and repairing pianos, as he was exempt from the draft
and soon to be married. C. F. Theodore's extraordinary talent for
acoustics and mechanics was well known. He was an excellent
and well-established pianist, who even at the age of fourteen had
performed on his father's instruments at the 1839 Brunswick
Music Fair, where the Steinweg pianos received an important
medal. He would eventually be responsible for forty-one of the
fifty-five patents issued to Steinway and Sons.

As soon as the rest of the Steinwegs had arrived in New York
and were settled in their downtown Manhattan apartment, Mr.
Steinweg made the very wise decision to send three of his sons
for three years to various piano manufacturing companies to
learn the language, the American way of life, and the American
way of building pianos.

On March 5, 1853 Steinway and Sons was founded on Varick
Street in New York. (They had anglicized their name from
Steinweg to Steinway.) As early as 1860, after tremendous
successes at exhibitions and fairs, the Steinways opened a new
factory between Fifty-second and Fifty-third Streets and Fourth
and Park Avenue, where 350 men produced thirty square pianos
and five grand pianos a week.

Tragedy struck the Steinway family in 1865. After years of
working virtually day and night, two of the sons, Charles and
Henry died within one year. The elder Steinway was just sixty-
eight years old, and the death of his sons was a tremendous blow
to him and his family.

Hearing this news C.F. Theodore, the oldest son, who had by
then moved his factory from Seesen to Brunswick and had
become very successful in Germany, sold his business to three of
his best workmen, Grotrian, Helfrich, and Schultz, and came to
America to work with his father and his brothers Wilhelm and
Albrecht.

In 1866 Steinway Hall, a concert hall seating two thousand
was opened on Fourteenth Street in New York City. It was the
city's major concert hall until 1891 when Carnegie Hall opened
its doors.

The Steinway branch in London opened the following year, and the Steinway factory in Hamburg, Germany, opened in 1880. Of course the joining of C. F. Theodore to the Steinway family team was a tremendous success. The Steinway concert grand soon became the favorite of the concert stage, triumphing over the Erard and Chickering grand pianos which had dominated the concert world till then.

The need for more strength in pianos, to withstand the bravura playing and virtuosity of the best artists, was a challenge Steinway mastered marvelously. They strove to consistently build pianos which had both strength and fine tonal quality. I am happy to be able to say that the present ownership of Steinway is fully dedicated to maintaining Steinway's long-standing reputation for building the world's best pianos.

I am often asked why, in my estimation, the Steinway is the best piano. Here are some of my answers to that question:

- Let's talk first of all about the soundboard, which is the "soul" of any piano. The Steinway soundboard is either a close-grained Alaskan sitka, or an Eastern-seaboard or European spruce—a wood which has unusual stability and vibrancy under stress. It is created like the soundboard of violins, to give a free and even response throughout the entire scale. It is so constructed as to be nine millimeters thick in the center and tapered to six millimeters as it approaches the rim and outer case. This design permits complete freedom of movement, displacing a greater amount of vibrations into the air and thereby creating a richer and more lasting tonal response as well as giving a tremendously wide range in tonal possibilities, from extreme pianissimos to super-forte. It gives a great artist the possibility of a very colorful performance.

- The ribs, which hold together the pieces of the soundboard, are made of durable, resinous sugar pine to assure strong and constant support of string *down-bearing*, the downward force the strings exert on the bridges and soundboard. Rib ends are hand-fitted into their mounting surfaces, virtually locking into the important soundboard crown.

- The bridges are made of hard-rock maple and are vertically laminated, capped with hard-rock maple planed to the individually determined height, lead-coated, and notched by skillful hands for each individual string. This design defies splitting.

- The rim and case are double-bent. Both inner rim and outer rim are bent and pressed together into one piece and in *one* operation. This unique, long-standing Steinway feature makes the piano as a whole unit a sounding body. All case components are fitted by hand, glued and maple-doweled for homogeneity before the installation of the soundboard. The rim is made entirely from hard rock maple, consisting of eighteen laminations for the smallest grand.

- There are five solid spruce braces (less in the smaller grands), maple-doweled into the rim and thus again creating a single, homogeneous foundation of one sounding unit.

- The action parts are anchored to a tubular metallic frame (another Steinway feature), fitted with a hard maple interior dowel which is force-fitted at minimum moisture content for stability in every climate.

- The hammers are cut from 100 percent virgin wool felt, containing no admixture of other materials. They are compression-wired for permanent shape before being individually voiced.

Steinway is the absolute standard in piano-building. This fact always becomes obvious as one goes to piano technician conventions and listens to teachers and instructors of piano technology who are not affiliated with Steinway. The durability and

A young Franz Mohr sits with Hupfer, the chief concert technician when Mohr joined Steinway and Sons in 1963. Hupfer was a legend, working with piano greats of his time.

An older Franz Mohr at work on a piano action in Steinway's famous "basement."

Franz Mohr overseeing the unpacking of Horowitz's piano on his last tour of Japan in June of 1983.

Franz assisting Horowitz in making sure the piano and bench are appropriately placed for the Maestro.

Photo by Masami Hotta

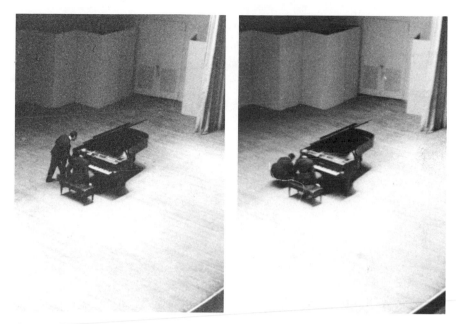

An interesting series of photos was taken from the balcony of Carnegie Hall at a Horowitz concert in the late sixties. Horowitz broke a string on his piano and could not continue to play. Franz saved the day by quickly going out on stage and replacing the string for the Maestro. Horowitz started the piece again as if nothing had happened.

Franz Mohr with Van Cliburn and Shura Cherkassky.

Basic parts of a Steinway piano action.

STEINWAY & SONS

GRAND PIANO – CROSS SECTION
MODEL – M

1 - KEYBED	47 - KNUCKLE
2 - KEYFRAME	48 - HAMMER
3 - KEYFRAME FRONT RAIL	49 - UNDERLEVER FRAME
4 - KEYFRAME FRONT RAIL PIN	50 - UNDERLEVER FFRAME SPRING
5 - KEYFRAME FRONT RAIL PUNCHING	50A - UNDERLEVER FRAME SPRING PUNCHING
6 - BALANCE RAIL	51 - UNDERLEVER FRAME CUSHION
7 - BALANCE RAIL STUD	52 - UNDERLEVER FLANGE
8 - BALANCE RAIL PIN	53 - UNDERLEVER
9 - BALANCE RAIL BEARING	53A - UNDERLEVER LEAD
9A - BALANCE RAIL BEARING STRIP	54 - UNDERLEVER TOP FLANGE
10 - BACK RAIL	55 - DAMPER WIRE SCREW
11 - BACK RAIL CLOTH	56 - TAB
12 - KEY STOP RAIL PROP	57 - DAMPER STOP RAIL
12A - KEY STOP RAIL PROP BLOCK	58 - DAMPER WIRE
13 - KEY STOP RAIL	59 - DAMPER GUIDE RAIL
14 - DAG	60 - DAMPER HEAD
15 - KEY	61 - DAMPER FELTS
15A - KEY LEAD	62 - STRING
16 - KEY COVERING	62A - STRING REST FELT
17 - SHARP	63 - AGRAFFE
18 - FRONT PIN BUSHING	64 - TUNING PINS
19 - KEY BUTTON	65 - SOSTENUTO ROD
20 - BALANCE PIN BUSHING	66 - SOSTENUTO BRACKET
21 - CAPSTAN SCREW	
22 - BACKCHECK	67 - KEYSLIP
23 - BACKCHECK WIRE	68 - KEYBLOCK
24 - UNDERLEVER KEY CUSHION	69 - KEYLID
25 - ACTION HANGER	69A - KEYLID PIVOT PLATE
26 - SUPPORT RAIL	70 - CASE CORNICE
27 - SUPPORT FLANGE	70A - CASE CORNICE LIP
28 - SUPPORT	71 - WRESTPLANK
29 - SUPPORT CUSHION	72 - PLATE FELT
30 - FLY	73 - PLATE
31 - TENDER	74 - NOSEBOLT NUT
32 - FLY REGULATING SCREW	75 - LAG SCREW
33 - SPOON	76 - DOWEL
34 - SUPPORT TOP FLANGE	77 - HITCH PIN
35 - BALANCIER	78 - DUPLEX SCALE
36 - BALANCIER REGULATING SCREW	79 - BRIDGE PIN
37 - REPETITION SPRING	80 - BRIDGE
38 - REPETITION FELT BLOCK	81 - SOUNDBOARD
39 - BALANCIER COVERING	82 - RIBS
40 - HAMMER REST	83 - FRONT RAIL
41 - REGULATING RAIL	84 - CROSSBLOCK, SPRUCE
42 - LETOFF SCREW	85 - CROSSBLOCK, BIRCH
43 - HAMMER RAIL	86 - BOTTOM BRIDGE
44 - HAMMERSHANK FLANGE	87 - LYRE TOP BLOCK
45 - DROP SCREW	87A - LYRE PILLAR
46 - HAMMERSHANK	87B - LYRE BOX
	87C - LYRE BOTTOM
87D - LYRE STICK	100 - OUTER RIM
87E - LYRE ROD GUIDE	100A - INNER RIM
88 - PEDAL PLATE	101 - BRACE
88A - PEDAL	102 - TOP
88B - PEDAL CUSHION	102A - TOP BUTTON
89 - LYRE ROD	102B - TOP HINGE
89A - LYRE PEDAL ROD NUT	103 - TOPSLIP
90 - TRAPWORK LEVER	103A - TOPSLIP FELT
90A - TRAPWORK SPRING	103B - TOP CATCH
90B - LYRE ROD PUNCHING	104 - LOCKBAR
90C - DOWEL CUSHION	104A - LOCKBAR FELT
91 - TRAPWORK HOOK	104B - LOCKBAR BUTTONS
92 - TRAPWORK BLOCK	105 - DESKSLIDE
92A - TRAPWORK PIVOT PIN	106 - DESKFRAME
92B - TRAPWORK WASHER	106A - DESKFRAME STOP
93 - DAMPER LIFT DOWEL	107 - DESK
94 - CASTER	107A - DESK BUTTON
94A - CASTER SOCKET	107B - DESK HINGE
95 - LEG	107C - DESK PROP
95A - LEG TOP	108 - TOPSTICK
95B - LEG TOP BLOCK	108A - TOPSTICK PROP
96 - LEG PLATE	108B - TOPSTICK HINGE
96A - LEG PLATE PIN	108C - TOPSTICK BUTTON
97 - LEG BUTTON	
98 - CONSOLE	
99 - BACKBOTTOM	

Van Cliburn performs at the White House reception for the Japanese Emperor. Franz Mohr, wearing a hastily fashioned white tie, is seen between Betty Ford and the Emperor.

Franz Mohr with the White House Piano after his extensive over-hauling.

longevity of the Steinway piano, in striking contrast to mass-produced instruments always comes to light when old Steinways are rebuilt. My own Steinway at home is a 1921 Model O in mahogany and it is indeed like new, with a new soundboard, new strings, as well as a rebuilt action with new hammers. It is a magnificent, marvelous instrument with a beautiful tone. My son Michael, who is the National Director of Services at Steinway, rebuilt a mishandled 1890 Model A, which is a striking testimony to what can be done with an "old" Steinway. It is just beautiful, with a marvelous tone and action.

The story is told that when Vladimir Horowitz came to the doors of heaven, the angel in charge of music shouted to the harp-playing angels, "Put your harps away and roll out the Steinway: Horowitz is coming!"

8 Tuning a Piano

Let's talk about what is involved in tuning a piano. There is much misunderstanding about this process, but I'll try to put it into terms that anyone interested in this subject can understand. Tuning is extremely important as even the best-regulated piano is of no value whatsoever if it is out of tune. What is tuning? It is simply the stretching of a string to such a point that it vibrates at just the right pitch. The pitch of a concert grand piano is usually such that the middle A-string vibrates at 440 cycles per second.

Pitch

At the close of the 19th century an attempt was made to set a standard from among the various pitches then common. This was eventually achieved by the passing of the "French Resolution," which fixed the concert pitch at A=440 hertz (cycles per second). Unfortunately, in our present day there is no longer a universal agreement. Each orchestra sets its own pitch, anywhere between 440 cycles per second to 446. That often puts the concert piano tuner in a difficult situation.

A few years ago when the Dresden Symphony Orchestra was playing in Carnegie Hall, I had tuned the piano to 440, which was the standard pitch. I went to the rehearsal to see if the soloist was happy with the piano. As soon as the A was given there was quite a commotion, since that orchestra's pitch was 446. They declared that they could not perform on that "low" a pitch. I was given a half-hour to re-tune the whole piano to the 446 standard. Of course in such a short time it could not be an excellent tuning, but at least it was usable.

Another time, I was travelling with Rudolf Serkin and his famous piano CD 169 to several concerts. He had just played the Beethoven "Emperor Concerto" in Chicago with the Chicago Symphony. I had tuned the instrument to 442, since that was the pitch of the orchestra. The next concert was with the Cleveland Orchestra in Severance Hall a few days later. I was eager after the concert in Chicago to get to New York the next day, since Elisabeth and I had an invitation to Horowitz's birthday party at the home of Peter Gelb, his manager. Serkin had been so kind to release me for the two days. The agreement was that, since his piano stays so well in tune they would play the rehearsal in Cleveland without me tuning for it, but I would come in the early afternoon from New York to tune for the evening concert.

I got a call from my wonderful friend Daniel Majeske, the Cleveland Symphony Concert Master, just as I was leaving for the airport in New York. He was quite upset that the piano was at 442, and told me to make sure that the piano would be on 440 for the concert.

The Tuning Procedure

Briefly, here is the procedure we follow in tuning a piano. First the concert A, which is key 49 (or "A^4") is tuned, using a tuning fork as a reference point. We set what is called the "temperament" between A^4 and A^3, that is, key 49 and key 37. Setting the temperament in this octave is the foundation of the tuning process.

After tuning the octave A^4–A^3, we precede as follows:

1. A37 >>>> E44, a fifths
2. E44 <<<< B39, a fourths
3. B39 >>>> F#46, a fifths, check the sixths A–F#

4. F#46 <<<< C#41, a fourths, check the thirds A–C#
5. C#41 >>>> G#48, a fifths, check the sixths B–G#
6. G#48 <<<< D#43, a fourths, check the thirds B–D#
7. D#43 <<<< Bb 38, a fourths
8. Bb 38 >>>> F45, a fifths, check two thirds C#–F and F–A
9. F45 <<<< C40, a fourths, check 3rd C–E and check the sixths C–A
10. C40 >>>> G47, a fifths, check 3rd D#–G and check sixths Bb–G
11. G47 <<<< D42, a fourths, check two thirds D–F# and check Bb–D

One has to hear and know the sound pattern, or should I say the sound character of the thirds and the sixths in order to set a well-tuned temperament. The first four notes are the most important ones in the temperament. When they are set right one has eighty percent of the temperament, for the rest will fall into place.

Also remember that no fourth or fifth is tuned "pure." One has to temper in order that all intervals fit throughout the circle of fifths. All major thirds should fit into a smooth, ascending progression. Also, all major sixths should fit into a smooth, ascending progression. Starting from this middle octave all the rest of the piano is tuned in octaves, keeping in mind that octaves are tuned a little bit sharp, or wide.

It is very important that the concert tuner tune very solidly. By this I mean that the piano for a concert must be able to withstand a real beating. The concert pianist really hits the keyboard, so as tuners we have to tune in such a way that after the concert is over, the piano will still be in tune, in as fine a condition as it was before the concert. That *can* be achieved.

I always say that it is difficult to find a tuner who tunes on a high level of workmanship, but that it is even more difficult to find among those who tune very well, one who also tunes solidly—so solid that the piano can really take a beating in the concert and still be in tune. One can only become a solid tuner by working on it constantly, and by never losing sight of the fact that this piano is going to be used for a concert. No tuner should ever take the tuning hammer off of the pin he or she is working on without being absolutely sure that this note, this string, will withstand the strongest beating, and will not budge in any way. This takes time!

I am always being asked about the value of using what is called a "strobe" tuner, which is an electronic tuning device for tuning a piano. I know that many tuners today use this device, especially in the United States, though not so much in Europe. I am personally dead set against it. I am against it for a number of reasons.

The first reason is that, although the machine itself is absolutely perfect in showing you the right pitch, it is quite another thing to translate, or to transform what the machine is telling you, into the tuning itself. It is not possible to develop an ear for skilled tuning without the training which comes with years of developing extremely fine feeling in one's hands. That sense of feeling enables one's hands to set a tuning pin, or to set a string in such a way that gives one-hundred-percent assurance (an assurance only one's ears can tell) that this note is in, and that this note will not go out of tune no matter how hard it is hit. This is something which can never be done with a machine, because one who tunes with a machine relies on his or her eyesight as to what the machine is telling them to do. The information goes through the "eye gate," but that will never develop the feeling, this extremely sensitive, fine feeling which comes through the touch of your fingers, combined with the recognition of your ears, your keen hearing, to achieve this solid tuning. Through all my years of tuning, through all my years of training other tuners, I have never found a tuner who is able to do a truly good, skilled tuning using an electronic tuning machine.

Someone might ask, "What about using a strobe tuner for tuning a harp?" That is an entirely different matter. The tension in a harp string is nowhere near as great as in a piano string. The tension in a piano string in extremely high. The slightest movement of a fraction of a millimeter of a tuning pin makes a big difference in pitch in a piano string. Not so with a harp. Therefore there is no problem in using the machine in the tuning of a harp, because the margin in the tension is so much wider than with a piano string.

Another important consideration for concert tuners is proper use of the time available for tuning. Often there has been no time left for the tuner to do his work before a concert. Let us say the rehearsal has gone on far too long, and there is only a half-hour left before they let people into the hall to look for their seats. I must now not only know how to work very fast, but also just how to divide my time correctly to get my job done.

In a normal situation I have at least a half-hour, but even then I cannot do the most perfect job. I really need forty-five minutes to do a good job tuning the piano. I have seen tuners with such a drive of perfection that they would spend an entire day trying to set the most perfect temperament, then discover that they have no time left for the rest of the piano! It is difficult to find people who know how to pace themselves in getting the job done in the amount of time they have. To me this is one of the most important things to learn.

Of course a situation can arise in which one can do nothing whatsoever. Let us say you are given only ten minutes for tuning a piano which is out of tune completely. This is an impossibility. It has happened only once to me. Arturo Benedetti Michelangeli, the great Italian pianist, is the very opposite of Horowitz when it comes to practice times. Horowitz never would practice on the day of his performance. Michelangeli practiced every available minute, including the day of the performance. And, if he didn't feel just right about his last-minute practice, then he canceled!

The first time Michelangeli came to America—it must have been about twenty years ago—he didn't like any of the pianos we had in our Steinway basement, and went out to the factory with me to look at a new Steinway—CD 15, a piano that I personally loved very much. (That was more than twenty years ago. It was then with the Cleveland Orchestra for many years. Later, Edith Schaeffer will tell you the story of where it is now and of how I rebuilt it. It is an excellent instrument.) We brought CD 15 to Carnegie Hall for Michelangeli, and he practiced on it all morning the day of the concert. Of course a new piano doesn't stay in tune that well, and needs quite a bit of tuning before it is solid and can be performed on, so I begged him to please give me time for tuning. But after a break of only a few minutes at lunch, he began to practice and went on all afternoon.

"Maestro," I begged, "I would love to have a couple of hours to tune the piano, because it is a new instrument and the strings have not settled yet; one really needs to have a good amount of time to tune a piano, especially when it is new."

Well, he would not listen to me, or even look at me! He just went on practicing and practicing. The time got shorter and shorter. In my desperation I went to the Stage Manager, at that time Stewart Warkow. He helped me, and we both talked to Maestro. But he just said he had to practice, and would not leave the stage.

Finally I was down to a half-hour, and I still would have been able to do something in a half-hour. I begged him, and I begged Stewart Warkow. Stewart went again to Michelangeli and said, "We have to open the house in half-an-hour, and Franz needs half-an-hour to tune . . ."

But Michelangeli still would not listen—he had to practice.

By that time they had to open the doors, since they were already running late. Suddenly Michelangeli looked up at me and said, "I give you ten minutes . . ." and turning to the others he continued, ". . . *then* you can open the door and let the people in!" And he turned to go to his dressing room to put on his tuxedo for the concert. By that time I was rather upset, so I said to him, "Maestro, I warned you again and again that I needed *time* and now you give me ten minutes. I will not *touch* your piano!"

He played his whole concert on that out-of-tune piano. The next day a New York paper said it was too bad, at the Carnegie concert, that "Maestro's Steinway was out of tune!"

When discussing tuning, there is a need to be reminded again that pianos differ from each other; they "behave" differently. Some Steinway pianos stay solidly in tune no matter what, while others go more quickly out of tune, and need special attention. For instance Horowitz's piano, which he travelled with for the last years, is a piano which stays very well in tune. It can travel by truck or plane and still be in tune when it gets there, wherever it is going, across land or sea. We had it flown from New York to Japan. I tuned it before packing it in the box. When it arrived in Japan and we took it out of the box, it was still in tune. Other pianos are more sensitive to change and do not stay so well in tune. I really don't know why. Some people think that when they move a piano a few inches one way or another in their homes they need to call a piano tuner, because it will immediately be out of tune. We move pianos every day, shorter or longer distances, and they don't go out of tune.

A well-seasoned piano can even withstand substantial changes in temperature. For instance, suppose we tune a piano before it is taken to Lincoln Center or Carnegie for a concert on Saturday. The piano may be picked up from the basement and put on the truck on Friday, and stay on the truck all night to be delivered in the morning. We do not have heated trucks, so if it is winter the piano will be ice cold, and terribly out of tune, when it arrives on stage. But then an amazing thing happens: As the piano gets used to the surrounding temperature and warms up, it goes back into tune! It always amazes me how much a piano can take when it comes to changes in temperature or being moved.

Of course temperature *can* affect the tuning, especially sudden temperature changes in a new piano, where all the components—the wood, strings, and metal—are not settled. It takes time for everything to settle into place. The more consistent the temperature of the place where a piano stays permanently, the better it will remain in tune. The very best place I can think of for a piano is the Metropolitan Museum in New York City. They have a very sophisticated climate control system there, where several times a day the temperature and humidity is checked and controlled. The pianos there hardly ever go out of tune. For Steinway pianos in private homes, I recommend keeping the temperature as consistent as possible, and keeping them on an inside wall, away from windows or radiators. When those precautions are taken, some pianos will need to be tuned only once a year, and even then only minimal tuning will be needed.

I recall a lady I have tuned for who has two beautiful Steinways, and I couldn't keep either one in tune, especially the one which sat closest to the large window in her music room. I kept telling her she needed to move it to an inside wall, but her music room was small and there was simply no place to move it to. Then she moved to a different house, with climate control and a completely different room arrangement. There was a large music room, large enough that neither piano had to be next to a window. And from then on, both pianos stayed in tune.

9 *Perfect Pitch*

I should say a word about "perfect pitch." Over the years, quite a number of people have claimed to me that they have perfect pitch. By perfect pitch I do not mean relative pitch. Relative pitch means that one can say out of the blue sky, "That is a B-flat" or, "That is a G-sharp" or, "That is a D . . . this is an A." *Perfect* pitch, on the other hand, would mean being able to say, without any reference point, that middle A is vibrating at 442 cycles per second, or that it is vibrating at 438. No one can do that without a reference point, which is the tuning fork. No one with their natural sense of hearing can differentiate between 440 or 438.

One person who claimed he had this kind of "perfect pitch" was Eugene Ormandy, the famous conductor of the Philadelphia Orchestra. I ran into trouble with him a couple of times—once when I was on tour with Emil Gilels in Philadelphia. I was to tune the piano at eight o'clock in the morning to be ready for a ten o'clock rehearsal. I had just started to tune when Gilels came in and said, "Franz, I have come early because I want you to tune the pitch much higher than 440, because the orchestra, when it is warmed up, always climbs up [which is true, as far as pitch is concerned], and I want to be on top of them. Can't you tune it higher?"

And you know me, always eager to help and satisfy people! I said, "I still have my German tuning fork [which at that time was set to 444]; I am happy to use that."

He was all excited and immediately said, "Franz, please tune it to 444!"

I had tuned the piano to 440, and was just establishing the

pitch to 444 when Ormandy walked in. (He always arrived early for rehearsals, much earlier than any of the musicians—that was the old European way.) He realized right away that I was tuning to a higher pitch, although, as I said, he couldn't have known it was exactly 444. But he did hear it was a higher pitch, and he became all excited, saying, "That is great! Tune it like that! I have always had a fight with my orchestra; they want to keep it low and I want a higher pitch." He kept on saying, "Put it there! Put it there!" So I tuned the piano to 444.

I will never forget that day. Ten o'clock came and the orchestra was all in place. I was the only one in the audience, back a few rows from the front. At exactly ten the rehearsal started, and of course Gilels was sitting at the piano about to play Beethoven's "Emperor." The soloist gave the A to the orchestra, and as soon as the A was given on that piano the oboe player jumped to his feet, shouting to Maestro Ormandy, "Maestro, we are not playing at such a high pitch! It is an impossibility! We will not play!"

For the longest time, Ormandy and Gilels stood frozen like statues—Ormandy standing at the podium, and Gilels sitting at the piano—just like statues . . . while this oboe player kept repeating, "We are not playing at such a high pitch."

Finally Ormandy, knowing that I was sitting down there in the audience, turned around and said to me, "I'm sorry, but the piano has to be put down for tonight."

Well, what could I do? I had learned a lesson. I learned that I must not listen to certain pianists or soloists or conductors who demand something which is not in agreement with the policies of the orchestra. So I tuned the piano down, resolving I would never make that mistake again.

A few years later I was again with Ormandy, in Avery Fisher Hall at Lincoln Center, again with the Philadelphia Orchestra. The rehearsal was at ten o'clock in the morning, and the soloist was Andre Watts. The piano had been shipped in early in the morning before the rehearsal, and I had not had time to tune it. I found that it was not 440 but was flat—about 438. So I went to Maestro Ormandy and said, "Maestro, I am very sorry but I have had no time to work on the piano, and it is flat. But don't worry, I will work on it all afternoon and it will be fine by tonight."

He was very nice about it and said, "Okay, that is fine."

So of course in the afternoon I tuned my piano and had it exactly on 440, knowing very well that the official pitch of the Philadelphia Orchestra was 440. Then came the evening concert. The situation was as you see it many times in an evening concert performance. First the orchestra plays an overture or a short piece, then the second piece is the piano concerto. This night as usual a few musicians left the stage to make room for the piano, then the piano was rolled out in front of the orchestra. Just before the men rolled that piano out onto the stage, Ormandy stopped and hit the middle A, and immediately turned mad and said to me, "What are you doing to me? This piano is more flat than it was this morning."

I was upset with him and a bit nervous, too, so I said, "Maestro, if this piano is flat to you, then you've got no ears!" I was really upset.

Of course he was mad at me, and in a rage he ran out in front of the orchestra and began the concert. I felt very bad about the way I had responded to him, but I knew I was absolutely right. In the morning the piano had been flat. In my afternoon's work I had tuned it to exactly 440 and the pitch was precise. For him to tell me that the piano was lower than it had been in the morning was absolutely not true. How can anyone out of the blue sky say, "This piano is flat," with no reference point?

But I repented of my anger and prayed, "Lord, forgive me. I should not have been angry with him concerning this."

Orchestra members told me later that Ormandy was so mad that he had turned to the orchestra and said, "This fellow will never tune for me again. I will make sure of that." Well, I felt very bad about it, because until that time I had had such a good relationship with Ormandy, and I didn't know what to do about it. Should I apologize? But I really couldn't, because I was absolutely sure I was right! So I simply let it go.

A few months later, Ormandy was in Carnegie Hall with

Horowitz, playing the Third Rachmaninoff Concerto. And of course as I was always Horowitz's tuner, I had tuned Horowitz's piano for that concert. So I was then with Ormandy again, and he was very nice to me. Obviously our earlier confrontation was forgotten.

I could tell you many other stories about people who claim they can have perfect pitch without a reference point, but I will tell this one about Horowitz himself, who always claimed that he had perfect pitch. Many times he would say to me, "Franz, this piano is too high." He always wanted me to keep his piano at 440. I would never argue with Horowitz. I would simply say, "Maestro, it will be fine" or, "Maestro, I am sorry if it is a little bit high, you know, maybe it's the weather" . . . or whatever . . . "but it will be fine." Other times he would say, "Franz, the piano is low." He kept doing this all the time, but I never would argue with him.

Finally one day we were in Cleveland, and I bought him a tuning fork. "Maestro," I said, "I want you to carry this tuning fork, and I want you to check me on my pitch, on my tuning." You see, the tuning fork is the reference point. One has with the tuning fork a real reference point. It is like the difference between having a thermometer for measuring fever, and simply putting a hand on a person's head briefly and being dogmatic about the degree of fever.

So Horowitz took the tuning fork . . . but he never used it!

We were in Amsterdam once, I believe it was on May 24, 1987 for a concert in the Concertgebouw. Horowitz was having his concert on Sunday and his rehearsal on Saturday, as always. So at four o'clock Saturday afternoon, I had just finished tuning the piano and it was in good shape. Finally Horowitz walked on stage with his entourage around him and sat down at the piano. But before he touched the piano, he turned to all of us standing around and said, "You know what? Now I see the tremendous difference between the American Steinway and the Hamburg Steinway. Steinway gave me a piano in my suite in the hotel, which is *so* beautiful, and of course it is a German Steinway. Do you know why it is so beautiful? It is tuned to 435!"

Of course that is an impossibility. The pianos in Europe are always tuned much higher than in America. But I kept my mouth shut.

Richard Probst, Steinway's International Director at that time, was there in Amsterdam with us, and he tried to tell him: "Maestro," he said, "you must know it is the other way around." He wanted to tell Horowitz that the pianos in America are much lower than the German pianos, so that in fact it was quite the other way around. But he didn't get very far. Horowitz immediately went into a tremendous fit, yelling at the top of his voice to Probst: "You! You go back to New York! You have *no* idea about pianos, about pitch, you should sell cars . . . *used* cars! You should not have *anything* to do with pianos. There is the door. Go back to New York. I don't want to see you!"

He yelled at him in such a way that Probst didn't know what to do. He had never seen Horowitz in a fit like this. So he turned around and left the stage. That's exactly what he did. He didn't go back to New York, but he left for Hamburg, which was the next town we were going to. After the rehearsal on Saturday, when we were all having dinner together with Horowitz, Mr. Probst's chair was empty.

As Horowitz played his rehearsal the piano inspired him, and he went on playing for a couple of hours, which he rarely does at rehearsals. He was so happy with the piano that he completely forgot what had happened before. But when the rehearsal was over, I thought I needed to talk to him. As I was his tuner, I had to know what pitch he wanted me to tune his piano to. "Maestro," I said, "you know I am your tuner. Tomorrow I have all the time in the world, and I can tune your piano to any pitch you want; but you must tell me which pitch you want."

I assumed at that time that Horowitz must have realized he had been wrong, because the piano was so beautiful and he loved it. He said, "Franz, I tell you what, I want you to tune that piano to 439-and-a-half!!"

Well, I suppose that was close enough to perfect pitch!

A few weeks ago, while being interviewed by a former music critic of *The New York Times*, I said, "There is no such thing as perfect pitch." Immediately he cut me off and said, "I know a number of people who have perfect pitch! People who can determine without any reference point at all that, 'this is 441, or 444,' or whatever."

Well, I did not argue with him. I know now to simply leave such statements alone. However I am saying, no one can have that kind of perfect pitch. The tuning fork is the necessary reference point for determining pitch.

*   *   *

As Franz speaks of the need for a reference point to determine musical pitch, and how so many musicians do not see the need for such a reference point, I think of the many people in our world today who have no reference point for their dogmatic statements about ethics, morals, law, justice, right, wrong, evil, or good.

Most theories as to where the universe came from have one thing in common: That there was something there, such as electromagnetism or particles which by pure chance, plus billions of years, formed tremendously diverse combinations which are found in the cosmos and in our own planet today. Even so complex a thing as the human brain, say these theories, came into being by pure chance plus time.

Most philosophic teaching today assumes that there is no such thing as absolute truth. In this world view, there is nothing that remains fixed. Everything is in a state of flux; everything is relative. Reality becomes something within a person's mind, rather than something unchangeable, outside of one's mind.

To find an answer as to whether the middle A of a piano is on 440, it is necessary to have a reference point, and this is the tuning fork. The answer cannot be measured subjectively by one person's ear, and then fit in with the reality of the orchestra.

To search for a way of doing something about alarmingly "out of tune" medical ethics; alarming uncertainty as to how to determine ethics in law; how to have an answer for what is right and what is wrong as to morals; how to find a way of measuring justice concerning the use of drugs and alcohol; what is the correct content to teach children and teenagers about sex; what to do about the thousands of unborn babies adults kill every day—to search for an answer that is correct, without a reference point, without a "tuning fork," is simply impossible. The only possible result would be total chaos as each person lived by their own changing standards, measured only by their own imaginations.

The strings of a piano do vibrate with measurable cycles, whether a person knows the measure or not. Denying something in one's mind does not make it disappear. Truth is true, whether a person accepts that truth or not. Believing something does not make it true. Reality exists outside of the mind. There is a reference point by which to measure ethics, right and wrong, in every area of life.

The Bible says that the universe was created by a Creator; it didn't come into being by chance. And the Creator, who made man and woman in his image, did not remain silent toward those he created. He created them in his image to think, to verbalize, to be creative, to have ideas and to choose, to act into space and time, to have significance in history—and he spoke to them. He gave them a reference point immediately, so that they would have the possibility of measuring what they did as "right" or "wrong" against that reference point, that tuning fork!

The first "tuning fork," so to speak, the first reference point was simply one command. When that command was totally disregarded, and Adam and Eve made their choice without referring to the reference point, the result was a spoiled, abnormal history.

However, the human race was not left without a true, unchangeable "tuning fork." We were not left to wallow in the chaos of shifting sand, trying to find a basis for ethics without any reference point.

I was talking about this on the phone with one of today's great pianists who is searching for God. Suddenly he said, "Oh, I see: You are saying that the Bible is the reference point; the unchanging Bible is the tuning fork!"

Yes, Maestro, that is it!

With the Bible in hand, with the Ten Commandments in hand, one has a tuning fork that will not change yet will never be obsolete. The Creator of the universe, the one true God who made people in his image, knows who human beings really are, and what is right and wrong in their minds as well as in their spirits and in their actions. And he has given them a reference point, which is meant to be kept in hand, and used—to be read, and acted upon.

The final reality, and the final reference point, is God himself, revealed by the work of his hands: the entire creation; and the verbalized explanation he gave through the inspired writers of the Bible.

10 Regulating and Voicing a Piano

Regulating a piano refers to making the proper alignment of all the action parts, in such a way that the instrument can give its top performance. The action of a grand piano has more than five thousand parts, and many of those parts consist of wood and felt. Both wood and felt are subject to variables such as temperature and humidity. That is why we have to constantly regulate our concert pianos, which are moved all the time and are therefore subject to changes in temperature and humidity. Basically, all the moving parts in the action have to move freely, and yet have to be firm, without any side play.

Since the Steinway piano is not mass-produced, each one is different, feels different, and of course sounds different. There are, you must understand, 120 different jobs involved in building a Steinway piano—jobs done by very skilled craftsmen. Along the line in the making of each piano, each craftsman has left his own "mark" or personal skill in his work on that instrument. The result is a very individual instrument. This is absolutely marvelous when you consider that each individual pianist is also different, as all human beings are! Pianists are physically different, and have different preferences as to tone and action. Artists at the piano do not in any way sound like one recording being played over and over again, nor like a mechanical "player piano."

Earlier I spoke of visiting factories when I was in Japan with Horowitz, and expressed respect for their production of so many pianos. You will remember that the guide at the Yamaha factory said that they produce 800 pianos a day. It was staggering to see pianos as far as the eye could see in one immense hall. At Steinway in Queens we produce only about twelve pianos a day!

Many times when I am lecturing to piano technicians all over the country, some who have been trained by Yamaha get very very mad at me when I can't give them specifics concerning the regulation of a Steinway piano. But since there are a lot of variables involved in building the Steinway, each piano has to be handled differently, not only when it comes to tone, but also when it comes to regulation. It simply cannot be done by specific measurements or a mechanical rule. I always teach my technicians to be sensitive to each instrument. I say, "Let the instrument tell you what it needs, and go from there!" This gives opportunity for technicians to develop and use their individual talents, and to understand not only the difference in the pianos, but the difference in the artists' preferences and needs. After all, that is who they are regulating the pianos for.

For instance, as I have already pointed out, Horowitz would never have played an instrument which Artur Rubinstein would have preferred. Horowitz always needed a very responsive action. I mean by this an action which allows the keys to go down very easily at the slightest touch, and to have a tremendous "uplift" when going back to their rest position.

Rubinstein would never have played such an instrument. He needed an instrument with some resistance in the keys. He wanted to dig in, so to speak; he wanted to feel the resistance of the keys under his fingers.

It must also be said that when it comes to regulating an instrument, while it is important to allow a certain amount of freedom in "listening to the piano's needs," it is also of primary importance to be "even." That is to say a technician, in regulating the action, must be extremely even in all the regulating that has to be done. Some pianists might prefer a more shallow touch, others a deeper touch where the key goes further down—but whatever the technician must do for that particular pianist, it must be very even, so that the whole piano is in that same direction.

You have probably heard of the late Canadian pianist Glen Gould. His recording of Bach's "Goldberg Variations" became world famous. His recordings of Bach's 1742 collection of "Keyboard Exercises" became a part of the *Masterworks* recordings, and has been ever since. Gould, with whom I worked for many years, was a marvelous pianist. Hardly anyone could play Bach as Glen Gould could. I was very much involved with Gould for quite a time. I would go at least once a month to Toronto to work on his piano—not only to tune, but to regulate and voice it. Since he wanted such an extremely shallow touch it was a delicate job. As you give an instrument this shallow touch it is possible to go into a danger area, especially when there are changes in humidity and temperature. The danger is that all of a sudden the action cannot work.

Voicing

Let us say now that we have regulated a piano very well, and it is also in tune, then we can talk about "voicing" or "tone regulating." As a technician I am happy to work with a Steinway, because of the differences in each piano. Rather than doing a mechanical job, one has the opportunity to be creative as a craftsman. One has something under one's fingers, something one can work with, because each instrument wants to be handled differently and each artist wants something different. It is always such a challenge to me to get a new instrument under my fingers and to see the potential of that instrument.

Not every concert grand piano is a "big" instrument, suitable for big piano concertos such as Rachmaninoff or Tchaikovsky or Brahms. Some instruments cannot be made that brilliant in tone. Here comes the creativity of the piano technician. It is necessary to be able to see how one can build in tone in an instrument, to bring it to its top performance condition. Most of the instruments that come out of the factory are not immediately ready for the concert stage. Many times the instruments need to be "broken in," needing a bit of time before they are ready.

Perhaps one among ten new instruments I work on is immediately ready for the concert stage.

"Tone building" is such a sensitive area that the technician has to be a good musician, with good hearing, to be able to work on it. Once again I would say that each instrument needs to tell me individually what it really needs, for me to bring out the best that it is capable of. Let me put it another way: The soundboard of any given instrument has to tell me what it wants. You see, the soundboard is an extremely important part of an instrument. As I have expressed it, the soundboard is the very soul of the piano. The function of the soundboard is to pick up the sound of the vibrations of the strings and to greatly amplify those vibrations and release them into the air. The sound could never be generated simply by a hammer hitting at string.

Think about an electric guitar which is not amplified: When you just strike a string, there is hardly any sound at all. But an acoustic guitar, with its soundboard, or "sounding body" of wood—that is an entirely different story. When you strike a string the sounding body amplifies those vibrations and releases them into the air.

So you see, the soundboard is the soul of the piano. But not only the soundboard: The whole frame or "rim" of the piano is involved in producing the sound. It is all a part of the "sounding body." One cannot determine beforehand how a given soundboard will react to the pressure and tension of the strings—their tremendous "down-bearing" upon the bridge and soundboard. One piano can be extremely brilliant and also beautiful, while another has to be kept much more mellow to give its best. If I take a piano and try to force it beyond its capacity, because the pianist wants it to soar over the sound of the orchestra—if it does not have this potential, my forcing it will give a tone that is extremely ugly, harsh, and shattering. It would be more noise than tone.

I personally learned this lesson with strong force while working with Horowitz during the time of his "comeback" after thirteen years of absence from the concert stage. He played recitals in New York, Chicago, Boston, and Washington, then suddenly decided to play the Rachmaninoff Third Concerto with the New York Philharmonic. He was a good friend of Rachmaninoff. They had played together in the basement of the Steinway company many times. They worked together well.

As I said before, every artist has this tremendous fear: "Will I be heard over the orchestra?" Horowitz had that same fear, and he kept telling me, "Franz, I need *more* tone! I need *more* brilliance! My piano won't do! I will not be heard!"

So, I worked on his piano. I built up the tone. I made it as brilliant as I could—as brilliant as I could feel responsible for. And he brought the piano several times to Carnegie Hall to try it out. But he was still not happy. As a technician, as a tone regulator, I felt I could not go farther, otherwise I would be killing the tone rather than making it better.

But he forced me. He said over and over, "Franz, I need more tone."

So I said to Henry Steinway, "How can I do it? The tone is already so ugly, so harsh, so glassy. It is not a healthy piano tone."

And he replied, "Franz, you *have* to do it. You have to help him."

Well, I tell you . . . I did bring the tone up. I filed and lacquered the hammers. But the tone was ugly—so ugly that I could hardly stand the rehearsal. Yet Horowitz still was fearful of not being heard, and he even moved his piano into the middle of the orchestra (he can get away with that!), where he was surrounded by all the musicians. The violins and other strings were in front of him. He even had a platform made for the piano! I had never seen a piano in a position like that.

The night of the concert, the tone was ugly. When the recording came out, I was ashamed of myself. I have the recording at home but have never been able to listen to it all through. I said the other day, "I will sit down and listen to it this time." Less than ten minutes into it, I shut it off. It is that ugly. What I am saying is that one can go only so far in building tone in a piano; if you go farther it becomes unacceptable.

After that series of concerts, (he played the same concert with Zubin Mehta conducting the New York Philharmonic), Horowitz went into seclusion for some time; it was all quiet on Ninety-fourth Street. The piano stayed downstairs in the Steinway basement, and I took the responsibility for doing something which I felt I had to do! I took out all those hammers that I had filed and lacquered to make hard, and put new hammers in. I worked to build the tone in such a way that it would be brilliant, but still a good tone. And I weighed off the action in such a way that he would not know, as far as the spielart is concerned, that it was not the same action.

Then I called Horowitz and told him a "white lie." I said, "Maestro, I just opened your instrument, and it has changed quite a bit! You know, nobody plays your instrument down here. It has not been played now in some months, and it is much more mellow than you remember it. To me, it is beautiful, but I am terribly concerned. Why don't you come down sometime and look at it and tell me what we should do. I know that in the fall you are going to play some concerts, but you should come and look at your instrument."

Of course I saved all the old hammers, so that I could put them back if he did not like the change. I knew I was really taking a chance.

Horowitz always came to Steinway Hall when nobody else was there, always after hours. He was a very shy person, and he never wanted to see anyone whom he did not know personally. That night, a guard was there to let him in, and of course we were expecting him. We put that piano in the center of the room, right in the center of the famous Steinway Concert Basement. Horowitz came in, sat down, and played. He played and played. He stopped a moment, and he played some more. He stopped and said, "This is so beautiful! This is my instrument. This is the tone I want. This is the tone I am looking for." Then he went absolutely bananas! How beautiful this instrument was, he kept saying. How beautiful it was. It had changed to be its best!

The piano inspired him so much that he wanted to play again.

He said, "By the way, we are going to do some more concerts now."

Then I knew that I had been on the right track. I had done the right thing.

This, of course, is the instrument everybody knows now. This is the piano which we took to Moscow and which you hear in your home on the recordings made there. This is the piano that went to Milano for those recording sessions with Guilini conducting the Scala Orchestra, when Horowitz recorded Mozart's Piano Concerto No. 23 and his Sonata K333. This is also the piano we took on the second tour to Japan. This is the piano which you remember so well in his recordings, the piano that continues to be kept the same, even now after his death.

We keep Horowitz's piano the way it is now. But that whole incident showed me something extremely important—that when it comes to voicing a piano, I must use my own judgment, and not listen too much to the artist! If he or she is asking for more brilliance or tone, I must be very careful to do what I have to do, but only so far. I need to protect the performance. I need to protect the recording. And I need to protect myself too—because I am the one responsible for the tone.

In my travels with musicians all over the world, I have learned what happens when pianos are made too brilliant, so brilliant that they are harsh and glassy. This is done in many countries, but especially in Japan. It impressed me in Japan to see Steinway pianos (Hamburg Steinways) in all the major halls. I went to several concerts in Tokyo to see how our Japanese pianists work. As Horowitz always had his practice times on Saturday and his concerts on Sunday, I had much time on my hands to make observations. As I listened to those pianists who had such marvelous technique, playing on instruments that were voiced much too glassy and harsh, the performance became so extremely boring. You see, the playing on such an instrument loses its color. It is all on one level. A piano needs to give a wide range, from pianissimo to fortissimo, from the most delicate note, to crashing thunder! This was what Horowitz could do. I found none of this was among the pianists I heard in Japan.

In Moscow, as people were listening to Vladimir Horowitz playing on his beautiful piano, with its singing tone, one of the leading men from the state owned artists' management agency took me aside and said angrily, "Your company should really be ashamed of themselves, because the pianos they give us from Hamburg, the Hamburg Steinways, are so brilliant and so glassy, and now here comes Horowitz with such a beautiful instrument, and you give us such nasty, harsh instruments." Then he asked, "Can't you do something about it?"

I tried to tell those people in Moscow that, "This has nothing to do with the instrument itself. It is simply that the technician has made those instruments super-brilliant. And he probably did so on the demand of the artists."

I am so happy that Horowitz got away from that super-brilliant tone he had me prepare for him, to a piano which he loved so much after I had installed the new hammers. In Moscow and after that you can hear the beauty of this piano. Listen to his last recording, which I think is extremely beautiful. Or listen to *Horowitz at Home*, which is also an excellent recording. Deutsche Grammaphone wrote me a letter about that one, which I am very proud of. They simply said, "Franz, we thank you so much for the beautiful tone, the beautiful instrument which you prepared for Horowitz. Because without you, Horowitz could not have *made* such beautiful recordings."

*   *   *

What Franz is explaining about pianos having individual capacities, individual possibilities, is applicable to human beings as well. So often young people, or even older people, are pushed to do things beyond their capacity. The ambition or greediness of a parent or teacher or coach can push or force that person beyond his or her capacity or potential, resulting in something ugly rather than beautiful. To be pushed to be something one is not, carries the same danger.

The piano certainly is not driven by personal ambition to be something beyond its basic capacity or potential! The forcing or pushing that spoils the beauty of its voice has to be done by someone else—the technician, often because of pressure from the performer. Human beings, unlike pianos, often unfairly push themselves, because of their own personal ambition. The drive to be "first," or to be "heard above the rest" can turn into harshness and give a twisted, shrill, unpleasant note.

In contrast, the developing beauty of a potential that is really there gives an exciting promise of fulfillment ahead for that person or instrument. My husband preached a sermon, "No Little People," which spoke of the significance and importance of each human being. There is something each of us can do in this moment of history, in this set of circumstances, that no one else can do. To not be fulfilling that for which we do have a potential, is just as much a waste as to be making an ugly sound as we are forcing ourselves or are being forced in the wrong direction.

Only the Creator, the Living God, can fully understand our potential. He is the One who can prepare the body and soul of his instruments to fulfill the potential with which he has made us. He also has given us some warning instructions. We are not to trust in ourselves, but in him, the God of the Bible, the Creator: "Blessed is the man who trusts in the LORD, whose confidence is in him. He will be like a tree planted by the water that sends out its roots by the stream. . . . and never fails to bear fruit" (Jeremiah 17:7-8, NIV). In 2 Corinthians, when Paul had been flogged many times, in prison often, in shipwrecks and persecutions of all kinds, he asks the Lord to remove a new difficulty, which he describes as a "thorn in the flesh." But the Lord replies, "My grace is sufficient for you, for my power is made perfect in weakness" (12:9, NIV).

The promise, "As thy day, so shall thy strength be" (Deuteronomy 33:25, KJV) also fits in here. If we need strength to face tormenters in the desert, that is a special strength; but if we are ploughing a field, or painting a canvas, or playing a violin, in the midst of pain and tiredness, that is another kind of strength. We ask for what is needed, a moment at a time. As our Master Technician, our God knows us perfectly. He knows not only our potential, and how to "regulate" us to bring forth the best we could possibly do. He is also able to do that which is beyond the most expert piano technician: He can supply his strength in our weak spots, and he can fit us into the orchestra (into space-time history) to do that which no other instrument could do.

Each human being who comes to God the Father, through his appointed way, and then time after time places himself or herself into the hands of the Master of our souls, bowing before him, worshiping him and accepting his understanding of what "music" will be missing if we do not allow it to come forth from us—each human being who does that is consciously choosing to be and to do that which will most perfectly blend with the symphony.

PART 3

The Technician

11 Earlier Years

I was born on September 17, 1927, in a small village near Duren, which was the main town of Rheinland county, Germany. I was the second of three sons. My older brother, Tony, was born in 1925, and Peter was born in 1930. My dad worked at the post office. My earliest memories are of music. Dad loved to sing. He always sang after dinner, and during the long winter nights he would sing and play a variety of instruments. He played the guitar, the mandolin, and especially loved to play the zither, which is popular in southern Germany. He loved German folk music, but also the classical repertoire of Schubert, Mendelssohn, Mozart, and Beethoven. We had an old record player which had to be wound up. We listened to classical records as well as folk music and operas.

As there was constant music in our home, we naturally became familiar with the classics. Tony would sit for hours playing his accordion, singing various songs as well as arias from operas. We also learned many of the poems by Goethe and Schiller.

In 1930, when I was about three years old, Dad was given a promotion by the post office and we moved from our village to Duren. There we bought a one-family home, the realization of a dream for my parents. They had wanted so much to come to the city where there was so much more culturally than in the village.

Duren had a population of about 30,000 people at that time, and had a symphony orchestra, a symphony hall, and a theater, as well as several museums and other concert halls. I remember going to classical concerts with my parents. All the major artists of the day performed there.

Hitler came to power in 1933, when I was six years old, and

his Nazism slowly began to influence our lives. For instance, as young people we had to join the Hitler Youth Group when we were ten years old. I loved to go to the post office and walk home with Dad after work. One day as we walked home together, with Dad pushing his bicycle along, we saw a group of Nazi storm troopers marching toward us in their brown uniforms, carrying the swastika flag. I began wondering what Dad would do. I knew how he hated the Nazis. Often at home he would tell us, "This Hitler will bring us into war, and it will mean disaster for Germany." Many times he would say, "God help Germany."

So I was wondering what Dad would do, as it was a rule that everyone should stop and salute the flag and the storm troopers marching by. Everyone else was now standing at attention as this group passed us. I watched Dad stiffen up and begin walking faster, with a stern look on his face. His hands clutched the handlebars of the bicycle as he walked on, completely ignoring the flag and the troops. The leader of the troop came toward Dad yelling, "Why do you not salute the flag?" Dad said nothing. He simply began walking at a faster and faster pace. I had to run to keep up with him. The troop leader seemed not to know what to do, so he just shook his head and walked back to take his place in the march. *He probably didn't want to get too far behind,* I thought to myself.

War finally broke out on September 1, 1939, just before my twelfth birthday. Dad said, "Franz, under Hitler war was unavoidable. However, I am happy you are so young; you will not get into the army. The war will be over, and you will never have to join the Nazi army." But the war dragged on and on and on. It would be a long war, and each of us was going to be greatly affected in one way or another.

Some of Dad's good friends were Jews. We called the Jewish butcher "Uncle Ben"; the Jewish lady who ran the local grocery store was also a friend. After learning that Jews were being put into camps, Dad would often quote from Zechariah 2:8 (KJV)—"He that toucheth you toucheth the apple of his eye"—and would then say, "This is the end of Germany."

One vivid incident would stay with me all my life. One day our local railroad station was sealed off from traffic by the police and soldiers. As young kids we knew our way around, and were of course curious as to what was going on. We sneaked across the railroad tracks and climbed over some embankments. As we watched we saw truckloads of Jewish people being brought into the station, where they were forced into trains. We saw families being separated. It was a frightening and heart-rending sight. There was weeping and embracing as the soldiers pulled people apart from each other. I have never forgotten those scenes; it was terrible to see.

Later, reporting it to my parents, I said, "The way those people said goodbye to each other, they must absolutely know that they will never come back here again." Mother prepared some sandwiches and Dad said, "Here, take these and see if you can get them to my friend Ben [the butcher], at the station."

Along with a friend I ran back toward the station. We found an old abandoned factory by the river. The river side of the building was unguarded as there was a locked door on that side. There wasn't much foothold but we climbed up and made it to a broken window. We could see people packed together, waiting; one man was wearing his yarmulke and prayer shawl and was holding a burning candle. As we listened, breathless, he quoted from Psalm 121: "I will lift up mine eyes unto the hills, from whence cometh my help. My help cometh from the LORD, which made heaven and earth" (verses 1–2, KJV). After the psalm was finished we passed in the package of food with Uncle Ben's name printed on it. We jumped down and got away without being caught by the soldiers, then ran home, weeping with terror and sorrow. What would happen to our friends and all the others?

Soon after that, Tony was drafted. We went to the railroad station to say goodbye to him. Each of us in our own way knew we would never see him again. And we never did.

For as long as I can remember I had wanted to be a musician. There was nothing I wanted to do with my life except to become a performing artist. My dream was to play the violin. When I was very young my parents provided me with the best teacher they knew of, Mr. Apel, who was the concertmaster of the local symphony orchestra. He was so thrilled with the speed of my learning and skill in mastering the violin that he encouraged my father constantly to send me as soon as possible to the Music Hochschule at the University of Cologne. Unfortunately my music education fell into the difficult time of the war, when everything changed.

Along with other teenagers I traveled daily by train from Duren to Cologne, twenty-five miles away. There was a brother and sister, Hubert and Resi, children of the local violin maker, who spent hours with me playing chamber music. Hubert played the piano and violin, and Resi was studying cello. There was Gunther Schmitz, a gifted violinist, and Franz Joseph Schetter, who was a pianist and was studying music composition. We played together every Thursday night. These are wonderful memories. We played all the Haydn string quartets, for which I switched over to playing viola. Actually I made the viola my main instrument, as I did better on it than on the violin. We played almost anything we could get our hands on. We gave concerts in that time too, and our group became known. We had no idea how suddenly this short period of joyous music performance together was to end.

War activities were increasing. There were bombings of our cities. Cologne was bombed, and train service was often interrupted, so that it took hours to get to school. Then everything came to a swift halt. It was a spring morning in 1943; we were on the train going to school. After some delays we came to our stop, only to find that our building was half destroyed and our beautiful auditorium was on fire. So many concerts had taken place there and the organ had been especially famous. Now as we stood there horrified, the organ sent out grotesque disharmonies as its pipes were activated by the fire's flames and by hot bursts of air. Its terrible sound became weaker and weaker, with an unbelievable groaning, almost human.

That was the end of our going to school. The invasion had taken place and the Allied troops were advancing; some of them

were within fifteen miles of Duren. As the artillery began
shelling our beloved Duren, we spent almost all of our time in
our air-raid shelter. We had reinforced the walls of the shelter,
building an emergency exit into the yard with a heavy steel door,
with two big handles like you find on a submarine.

Then came November 16, 1944—the day our city died.

Let me describe that day the way I saw it as a seventeen-year-
old boy. It was early afternoon, November 16, and it all took
place in just twenty minutes. Just before it happened, I did
something I had never done before: I climbed up and sat on the
roof of our house (situated on the outskirts of the city), watching the sky. Why? It is hard to explain. Sometimes we have a
deep premonition in our hearts, knowing something terrible is
going to happen.

We had become used to living with constant air raids. When
there were lulls in the artillery barrages we would come up out
of the shelter and do some cooking and eating in the kitchen;
these hasty meals were often interrupted by more artillery fire,
sending us back down to the shelter. At night the sky would
light up as search lights scanned the sky looking for planes. And
when the lights would lock on a plane, anti-aircraft guns would
bring it down. I would look at the sky and count the planes
falling and bursting into flames.

There was something else that made me sit on the roof watching the sky that November 16th: We had rabbits and chickens in
the backyard, and as I had tried to feed the chickens that day,
they all huddled together in a corner and wouldn't eat. Then as I
threw food into the rabbits' cages, they too huddled in a corner
and refused to eat. This added to our sense that something was
going to happen.

Many of the people in our town had already evacuated their
homes and gone toward the east. My father felt that we would
be better off to stay in the city, because the allied troops were
advancing from the west: He said it would be better to fall into
the hands of the Americans than into the hands of the Russians.

Now, as I sat on the rooftop on that dull, cold November day
after breakfast, Dad said, "Let me get the bicycles ready, and then

we can ride to our old home village [about ten miles away] and stay with some relatives. We can stay a day or two there." Meanwhile my mother was preparing a quick lunch, and then we were going to leave. I was still sitting on the roof when suddenly I saw B-17s approaching our city from the west— planes, planes, planes, as far as my eyes could see, flying at a very low altitude with the roaring growing louder all the time. I saw the first plane throw a smoke signal and I knew it was for us. I ran down the stairs yelling at my parents to run into our shelter.

What happened in the next few minutes we would only later begin to comprehend. We had just closed and locked the fire door in our shelter when the bombs began to fall. We were sure that this was the end for all of us. Mother started to cry out to God for deliverance and protection. There was a lull in the bombing and, thinking it was over, we opened the door. It is hard to describe what I saw as I stepped outside. One side of our house was heavily damaged, with a big crack showing the staircase hanging crookedly. There was an extreme heat like a furnace, with a strong wind sweeping through the streets igniting one house after another. There was a thick yellow burning, liquid napalm, or phosphorus, from the firebombs. I watched as people were caught in it, burning up right there before my eyes.

But the bombing was not over. There were other waves of planes roaring toward us, unloading their bombs with death and terror following. I ran back into our greatly damaged house. The upstairs was now on fire, but we made it down into the shelter and closed the doors again. Bombs were exploding all around us, and then suddenly the house was directly hit. Those moments are undescribable. My mother cried out to God again. All of a sudden, listening to her, something inside me snapped. I cried out, "Mom, shut up! There is no God! There will be no protection! There will be no deliverance! If there is any God, how can he allow something so terrible? No, there is no deliverance. We will all die together like cattle right here."

And I went on yelling, becoming totally irrational. I put my hands over Mother's mouth to stop her words, crying out, "Shut up, Mother, shut up, Mom, no . . . no God!"

In the moments after that deathblow came to the house, and everything was falling and burning, I saw a hole open just above me. I clawed and pulled myself out, the burning pain shutting out thoughts of anyone else. I began to run from the terrible inferno, my skin burned, bloody patches all over my face. As I ran I grabbed my hair at one point, and it came off in my hand, as a wig or a hairpiece would come off. I kept on running. My eyes hurt so much I could hardly keep them open. Yet I still had my legs, my arms, my hands. I could still climb over walls and keep going. Going where? No idea, just running. No one could tell where streets used to be. The city seemed turned upside down and upside down again.

Later we learned that in just twenty minutes of bombardment, 24,000 people had died—98 percent of all who were living there at the time. (Four or five thousand had evacuated before the bombing.) Only a handful escaped alive. Some died after days of being trapped in the rubble and ruins of houses.

Our city was in a valley. As I continued pushing my way up the hill, I looked back at the city. All the fires of the town seemed to be joined together, with the smoke going up in one single column. I suddenly thought of Sodom and Gomorrah in the Bible, where Abraham looked at Sodom the next day, "And behold the smoke from that city went up like smoke from an oven." That is what Duren looked like to me.

As I ran to escape, I saw dead people lying all along the way. One man was pushing a bicycle up the hill with a dead body tied to it, probably one of his relatives. I saw dead and some wounded on pushcarts, and people who were hurt, dragging themselves along in a kind of stupor. I was shocked at the bleeding and dying.

Somehow I made it all the way to the village where I had been born. Some farmers found me on their doorstep and took me in. I found out later that I then slept for a week, without even awakening to eat!

After that ordeal my memory slowly came back, and with memory came questions. "Where is Mom? Where is Dad? Where is Peter?" Just before Christmas 1944 my mother and father and I found each other, but Peter never made it out of the inferno.

Dad and I decided to take bicycles and ride back to Duren to try to find our house, and to perhaps find out something about Peter. We were absolutely sure that he was dead, and that there was nothing we could really do, but we wanted to see. We rode the ten miles into town, to where our street was; but it was in such ruins, with fires still smoldering and a lot of heat, that we couldn't do anything. We were very sad, and had a restless desire to scout around the area a bit, so we said, "There's nothing we can do here; let's try make it to the front line."

Tanks and soldiers were all over the countryside. As we went on some soldiers stopped us, asking where we were going. When they heard that we wanted to look for Peter, they let us go on. We made it to the river which goes through our town. The "front" had come to a halt there. On the west side were the Americans, and on the east side were the Germans. But on that day it was all quiet. There were no machine guns being fired, no artillery or air activity . . . for it was just before Christmas.

As darkness fell on that cold, foggy December night, all of a sudden we heard in the stillness a single trumpet, coming from the American side, playing with a very clear, strong, and beautiful tone, "Silent night, holy night, All is calm, all is bright." We were deeply moved, and began to quietly sing along.

When the last note died out, another trumpet began to play, this time from the German lines, almost next to us. This trumpet sound also was very clear and beautiful, playing a famous German tune:

> Ich hatt' einen Kameraden,
> Einen besseren findst Du nicht.
> Die Trommel schlug zum streite,
> Er ging an meiner Seite,
> Im gleichen Schritt und Tritt,
> Im gleichen Schritt und Tritt

An aerial view of Duren after it was bombed in 1944.

Eine Kugel kam geflogen.
Gilt sie mir oder gilt sie Dir?
Ihn hat es weggerissen;
Er liegt zu meinen Fussen,
Als wars ein stuck von mir
Als wars ein stuck von mir.

Will mir die hand noch reichen,
Derweil ich eben lad.
Kann Dir die Hand nicht geben.
Bleib' Du im ew'gen Leben
Mein guter Kamerad,
Mein guter Kamerad

Here's the English translation:

I had a friend,
A better one you cannot find.
The drums called for action,
He walked at my side,
With the same determined step,
With the same determined step.

A bullet came flying.
Is it for me or for you?
It was he who was struck;
Now he is at my feet,
As if a part of myself,
As if a part of myself.

His hand is reaching out to me,
While I am loading my gun.
I'm so sorry, I can't grab your hand.
But in eternity you'll remain
My good friend,
My good friend.

After a long and moving silence, we grabbed our bikes, not

saying a word, and moved back away from the front line, thinking only how ugly war is. There was that little river, a front line, soldiers on both sides from families of fathers and mothers, sisters and brothers; far away from home, longing to be with their loved ones, especially at Christmas time; yet they were locked into a situation where the war was not over, and they were still going to have to kill each other.

Christmas 1944 was very sad indeed.

My parents had started going to church again, but I told them nothing would ever take me back to church. Something inside me had completely broken. I had come to a conclusion which I was sure would never change: "There is no God; if there was, how could he allow something so terrible?"

Then, after the war, truths even more terrible came out. Hitler had killed 6 million Jews. It was too much for me to digest. Many Americans will not believe me when I say that we did not know what had really happened to the Jews. My parents, who were devoted Catholics and very strong anti-Nazis, had always talked of how it was such a crime that Jews had been taken away from their homes and possessions and forced into concentration camps. We assumed that they were being made to work hard in those camps; but even my parents had a hard time believing that the Nazis had gone so far as to kill them.

Where was God in all this? I just wanted my music back! I wanted to forget what I had seen, and that we had lost all our possessions, and that all the people of the town were dead, and that we had lost Peter and Tony. I wanted to try and forget.

Right after Christmas, Dad and I went back to the house in Duren once again, hoping to find out something about Peter. The American forces had stopped by the river and would not move on again until February. Otherwise, it was a ghost town. We didn't see a soul. We located our house, now just a pile of twisted metal and smoking ruins. We had brought two shovels along with us, but what could we do with them?

There we stood with our shovels, our bicycles lying on their sides on top of the ruins. What were we going to do? Where could we dig? Suddenly in the stillness there was a noise in the smoldering ruins, and my father's voice echoed in the quietness, shouting, "Is someone there? Is someone there?" We listened and listened. We heard a very faint noise. Somebody, somewhere in all those ruins around us was still alive. I don't know how long we stood there, completely in shock, not knowing what to do or where to start. All of a sudden Dad grabbed his bike, and in deep desperation said, "We go home."

In April we went back to the house once again with some friends. We finally made it through the rubble down to the shelter, where we found six bodies totally charred beyond recognition. The bodies were so fragile that each one collapsed as soon as we touched it. We had brought our bicycles and a small pushcart with us. The pushcart contained a crudely made coffin, because we were determined to give Peter's remains a proper burial. We shoveled all the remains into one sack and put the sack into the coffin.

By then there was much activity in Duren. The Americans had bulldozed a wide "road" from west to east through the wreckage of the town. Troops were moving down the street, and one American military policeman stood in front of what used to be our house, directing traffic. Suddenly he looked up at us, and when he realized what we were doing, he came up on the mound of rubbish and with tears streaming down his face embraced Dad and me as we wept together, showing us love and understanding. Then, shaking his head, not saying a word, he went back down to his jeep on the side of the road, and went on doing his business. As for us, we went ahead and dug out six or seven bodies—knowing that Peter was among them. The bodies were totally charcoaled and unrecognizable, only fractions of their original size. At that time there were huge mass graves, and they are still there. Later, monuments were put up with the names of those who died in that air raid.

Slowly our town became free of the rubbish and ruins, and people came back and tried to make a living again. The Americans fed us and gave us drinking water in the beginning. They put all of us young people into working brigades. Our job was to bury all the dead bodies of both people and animals. I will never forget the indescribable stench. It was spring—April and May—and getting warm, and the air was filled with the stench of decomposing flesh! The Americans would give each of us half a bottle of whiskey so that we could function as we carried out this grisly task.

The cleanup work was going on all over the city. There were destroyed tanks, ammunition, war materials lying around everywhere. As people worked to clear them away, we often heard loud detonations of unexploded ammunition; many lives were lost and many were wounded while working on the cleanup. Twisted metal, piles of bricks and stones, and heaps made by bulldozing were being shoveled into railroad cars and taken to dump outside the city. Along with the stench and horror of death was the terrible sight of hills being formed outside the town, made up of what used to be homes and churches and stores. Today the town is beautifully rebuilt. Those hills are covered with grass and trees, hiding what is underneath.

Among those coming back to Duren was the family of two of my music playing friends, Hubert and Resi Sistig. Their father was the violin maker. Only the walls of their house were standing. We began to help them rebuild. However before touching the house, the first thing we did was search for the violins! Before the bombings, Mr. Sistig had prepared some big, airtight drums in which he had placed some violins and his violin-making tools. He had buried the drums as deeply as he could in the back yard. As we began to dig, it was exciting to find that although the yard had been ploughed over time and again by grenades and shells, the drums were intact and the instruments had survived. We were overwhelmed with joy that we could start to make music again. It was truly a gift of beauty from ashes.

My remaining friends and I founded an association called Music Friends of Duren. We started to play some concerts in schools and auditoriums which were usable. Even without windows and roofs, we made music. Some American soldiers found that we had also started a "Dixieland" band, and could play dance music. They supplied us with some instruments. I played in the guitar section, and we began to play for the Americans. So, while many Germans were starving, we had plenty to eat and drink because the Americans took such good care of us. Finally, in 1948-49, things began to normalize, and my friends went back to their conservatory of music, while I went to study at the Northwest German Music Academy in Detmold.

12 Out with the Old, In with the New

When I was young I often had trouble sleeping. There were questions that troubled me for a long time, such as, where do we really come from? And, what happens when we die? My father came into my room and found me awake one of these nights and asked, "Franz, why don't you sleep?"

I said, "Father, explain to me eternity. How long is eternity?"

Although I was so very young, Father saw how serious I was and sat down on my bed to explain. "Franz, imagine a huge, huge mountain, and that there is a bird which comes just once every year, and in its beak it carries away a pebble or some bit of earth from that mountain. When that mountain is all carried away after millions and millions of years, maybe then *one day* of eternity has gone by."

I never forgot that story. I wanted so much to live for eternity. Many times I thought, *What is our life, really? Why, even if we live to be a hundred years old, what is that compared to eternity?* I became an altar boy in the Roman Catholic Church and many times thought that maybe I should go into a monastery and pray and prepare for eternity. I also dreamed of a life of music, and of getting married and having a family. Yet deep in my heart was this desire to live and prepare for eternity.

Then the events of November 16, 1944, completely shattered my faith in God. I concluded that there was no God. How could anyone reconcile the existence of God with the reality of things like war? My heart became extremely bitter. I was filled with hate against the war which had shattered my world and my faith. I was filled with hate against the Nazis, who had started this whole mess. And the hatred increased as later I learned about their atrocities against the Jews. I saw war as a chain reaction of hate, hunger for power, greed, aggression, and retaliation. I thought, *If only someone would repay hate with love, then this whole war business would stop.*

I then became a friend of a devoted communist, who seemed to share my feelings. The matter of God seemed to be settled with him. He was an atheist. He kept telling me that only the communists and their philosophy would bring peace. I went with him to Communist Party meetings, and heard their slogans: "Workers of all nations unite." "We will bring peace." I thought to myself, *They must have the answer.*

All my communist friends were atheists. But I was not satisfied. I was not happy. Although I had come to the conclusion that there was no God, deep inside I felt there must be something altogether wrong with my thinking. My communist friends painted a bright future for me if I would just join the party and get involved with communist youth work. Somehow I always shied away from this, and never did become a member of the Communist Party.

Outwardly I was doing all right—playing in the band for the Americans; having enough to eat; even having our own car—but inside I was a mess. I had hundreds of questions, and no satisfying answers. No one I talked with could give me the answers I sought. Then one night a friend invited me to a home. "You are interested in English; why don't you come to meet this Englishman who is there tonight." As we walked into this home we found about a dozen people sitting around a kitchen table, some with Bibles open in front of them. The Englishman, a Dr. James McFarlane, seemed to be interested in me; but I was not interested in what he had to say, because I had made up my mind that there is no God and no hope for eternity. As I sat there I thought, "I have never met a more weird group of people." And I was very rude to this Englishman, but he seemed to ignore my rudeness. I tried to upset him, saying, "You are an Englishman. I am a German. You are my enemy. What are you talking about? Peace? There is no peace."

But he remained calm, and at one point said, "Franz, no matter how much hate you throw at me, I love you. And there is one who loves you more, and that is the Lord Jesus Christ. Your heart is on fire with tremendous hate, and only one can change it. That is the Lord Jesus."

To this day I can see Dr. McFarlane's face filled with love. He went on to say, "Franz, I want to give you a present. Here is a Bible. Let me put my name and address in it. Please write to me. I am going back to Cardiff, England, and I will be praying for you every day. I want you to know that all the honest questions you have will be answered. You will find answers in this book."

I honestly did not know how to handle this man. He was the first person I had ever met who repaid hate with love and understanding. I can still see his face so full of compassion. Although I did not want that Bible and had no interest in it, I could not bring myself to say no to his gift. I took the Bible home with me and put it on the shelf in my room. There was not much left to put in the room after the war. I had a shelf with a small radio and a few books, and I put the Bible there. I didn't open it, but in the back of my mind somehow I always thought, *There is that book.*

That evening, facing the Englishman, I was not interested in what he said; but there was something he read from the Bible that stayed in my memory and seemed to speak more loudly in the ensuing weeks and months. Although I didn't know where it came from at the time, what I remembered were the words of Jesus in Matthew 6:33: "Seek ye first the kingdom of God and his righteousness; and all these things shall be added unto you" (KJV). Many times I thought, *Wow! According to this, if someone has a relationship established with God, a vertical relationship, everything else will fall into place—all my questions will be answered.*

Whenever such thoughts came, however, I put them out of my mind, and time and again said, "There is no God; I have made up my mind." One day we got a letter from the Red Cross concerning Tony, my older brother, missing in war. They simply gave an address of one of the men in Tony's army unit, saying, "Why don't you contact this person to find out something about your son."

My parents and I went to Stolberg, near Aachen, to visit this comrade of Tony's. The young man had just come back from a Russian prison camp, and he told us, "I don't know much about Tony. The day we were taken prisoners by the Russians, Tony was marching along with us in a column. But that is the last time I saw him. I don't know anything else."

Then my parents sat down for a cup of coffee with this young man's parents, while the man took me into the back yard and said to me, "Franz, I want to tell you a little bit more about your brother. You can take it. You are a young man, but I didn't want to tell your parents. Tony was wounded that day when we had the last battle, and he could hardly walk. His comrades tried to drag him along at the back of the column, but they couldn't keep up with the rest of the prisoners, so they had to let him go and leave him by the wayside along with other wounded men. I didn't want to look, but we heard that some of the wounded ones were shot by the Russians right there. I am ninety-nine percent sure that Tony was one of them, killed right there beside the road."

How I hated what that war had done to us. But in the back of my mind was one ray of hope. There might be one door open for me. There, up on my shelf, was that Bible. I really was afraid to take it down to read, because the door of hope might then close!

It had been a year since the Bible had been given to me, when one day I took it down and thought I would give it a try. How do you read a book? Normally you start with page one. And this is what I did as I read that Bible. On page one I read the story of Creation, which I remembered from school days. Then there is the story of Cain and Abel. As I read about Cain's jealousy and hate, causing him to kill his brother Abel, it suddenly did something to me. I thought, *Here is the first family created by God, and in this family there is already war!* I began to realize that man is responsible for what he does by choice, and that I could not blame God for war.

I got quite excited and read on, until of course in chapter 6 I came to the account of Noah and the great Flood. I read that God looked and saw that the wickedness of man was great upon the face of the earth, that the earth was filled with corruption and violence. The Bible says God regretted that he had made mankind, so he brought a great judgment upon the earth. The Bible account says that only Noah and his family were saved, because Noah was a righteous man and found grace in God's eyes.

As I read on I found that God started again to populate the earth, using Noah's family. He started, so to speak, from scratch, just as he had with Adam and Eve. I stopped reading and said to myself, *We come out of God's hands, and in God's hands we will return, and what will it be?* I realized I could not blame God for the war. I saw that this earth was given to man by God, and that man by himself is responsible for taking care of the earth. We have done, and are doing, a terrible job with the earth.

I stopped reading the Scriptures at that time, but began to see the miserable life I was living. *One day I will stand before God,* I thought, *and I am not ready.* I saw that I was living a sinful life and would never make it to heaven. *I will work on myself,* I decided. *I will live a better life, and then go to God and simply say, "Please accept me."*

The more I tried to live a cleaner, more moral life, the more I simply fell into the same traps. The same things made me miserable. Finally I became desperate and said, "I can't make it; I can't live a better life." But I kept on searching. I started going to the Catholic Church with my parents. They were delighted. I went to talk to the priest and he simply told me to go through confession and all the other formalities; but although I tried to do that, many questions remained unanswered, such as, how does someone have the assurance that they are accepted by God?

Again there were sleepless nights. I talked to others about my thoughts, but nobody could help. The only thing that could calm down my nerves was smoking. I became a chain smoker, starting before breakfast each day.

By age nineteen I was in very bad shape physically. My stomach was severely damaged from the chain smoking. When I went to a doctor he said, "Some people smoke and it doesn't seem to bother them; they grow old smoking, and live to be in their nineties. But you cannot take it. It is harming your stomach. You must stop."

I tried many times to stop, but couldn't. I was already a piano tuner at that time and on one particular day was sent to a public school to tune six pianos. I was alone in the building; the caretaker had let me in and then gone home, saying he would come back later. I got such terrible stomach cramps that I couldn't go on with my work. The pain was so bad I was actually lying on the floor. Yet I couldn't give up smoking even though I knew the smoking was causing that pain.

One night I was feeling especially restless, smoking one cigarette after another while questions raced through my mind: *How can one live a better life? How can one get rid of tremendous hate, the kind of hate I have in my heart? Where could I find some people who would have the kind of compassion and love that the Englishman, Dr. McFarlane, had shown me that evening?* I went outdoors and walked for hours, finally coming home about 4:00 A.M. Light was just coming in the east. My room was upstairs and no one else was up on that floor. All of a sudden I thought, *My question about the existence of God is answered! There is a God! Man is responsible for everything on the face of this earth; each one is responsible for his acts; so that is answered, so why don't I pray?* I got quite excited about that idea. I thought, *Why didn't I think about that before?* So I got down on my knees beside my bed.

As I began to pray I wondered, *How do I address God, since I don't really know him?* I didn't want to use the prayers in the Catholic prayer book. They didn't suit me. They didn't seem to fit. So I thought, *How do I tell God how miserable I am? That I have wanted to live a better life but just can't make it? God, please give me an answer. Reveal yourself to me.* I wanted to pray like this, but could not bring one word out of my lips. Very strangely my thoughts were then drawn to the scene of Calvary where

Jesus died. I thought of the tremendous cry from his lips, "My God, my God, why hast thou forsaken me?" I thought, *If the Son of God was sinless, why did God forsake him and give him up?* I thought about the two criminals crucified with Jesus. I had not read the Bible for years and years, but somehow remembered that story. I am amazed today that everyone knows the story of the crucifixion of Jesus. All my Jewish friends know that story.

But that night by my bed, I thought of those two criminals cursing Jesus and crying, "If you are the Christ, the Messiah, why don't you come down from the cross and save yourself—and save us?" I remembered that one of those two men had a change of heart, and when the other one cursed Jesus again he said, "You should shut up; we are hanging here for the deeds we have done. But this man Jesus hasn't done anything wrong." And then he turned to Jesus and said, "Lord, remember me when you come into your kingdom."

You remember the story. Jesus turned to the man with tremendous compassion and love and said, "Verily I say, today you will be with me in paradise."

The tremendous truth became clear to me, although right then I did not know the exact words of 2 Corinthians 5:21: "He hath made him to be sin for us, who knew no sin; that we might be made the righteousness of God in him" (KJV). I didn't know the exact words, but did know that Jesus was made sin for that poor fellow who was dying on the cross beside him that day, and that he died for "whosoever would believe in him," so that they would not perish, but would have everlasting life (see John 3:16).

I was so overwhelmed by the love of God as it is revealed in Jesus Christ that I kept on saying, as I stayed on my knees that night, "Oh, thank you, Jesus; thank you very, very much." That's all I could do, I was so overwhelmed by what Jesus had done. "Thank you, Jesus; thank you."

I don't know how long I stayed there, but finally I lay down on the bed with all my clothes on and slept perhaps an hour—a deep, refreshing sleep.

My mother always made breakfast for me, and when I went

down that morning I said, "Mom, I had a sleepless night, but now I have peace in my heart. I became a Christian this night. My questions are answered in Jesus."

My poor parents didn't understand what I was talking about. "Franz, you have had all kinds of crazy ideas, and we kept quiet; we knew you had to find answers yourself. But you have always been a Christian, even those years when you were with the communists. You were baptized as a baby, and you are a Christian. You went away from the church, but you are a Christian."

They didn't understand, but I was so excited that I wanted to read more and more of the Bible. I decided to spend every spare minute reading the Bible. I resolved not even to read the newspaper until I had read all the Bible. I read late many nights. I read the Old Testament, then the New Testament. There were many things I didn't understand, but also many wonderful discoveries to get excited about. I was especially amazed when reading prophetic passages.

And I read, "If the Son therefore shall make you free, ye shall be free indeed" (John 8:36, KJV). I thought about the changes I had tried to make—like trying to change my hate to love—and how it didn't work. But now a change had come which only God could have brought. I read, "Therefore, if anyone is in Christ, he is a new creation; the old has gone, the new has come!" (2 Corinthians 5:17, NIV) I was sure I understood what was going on, and I tried to tell people about it; but nobody else seemed to understand. I thought I was the only Christian around!

My life was so drastically changed that it wasn't until some months later that I realized, *Wow! I haven't been smoking!* So many other things were exciting me in my discoveries from the Bible that I had completely forgotten about my long-time struggle with smoking!

I wrote to my friend Dr. McFarlane in England and told him what had happened. He wrote an exciting letter right back, saying, "You must know, Franz, that I have prayed for you all the time, every day."

I just marveled that this man to whom I had been so rude and had shown so much hate, had been praying for me ever since. I was overwhelmed that he was so filled with love and understanding.

I continued to read the Bible and talk confidently about salvation being a gift of God. ("For by grace you have been saved through faith; and that not of yourselves; it is the gift of God, not of works, lest anyone should boast"—Ephesians 2:8-9.) My parents became very upset that I would question the teaching of the Catholic Church. So one day there was a confrontation in our home, with my parents, our relatives, and the parish priest on one side and I alone on the other side! There were heated debates. At one point I declared, "If I would die right now, I would go right to heaven like that criminal who was crucified with Jesus, when he put his trust in him. Do you remember the story?"

That was too much. The priest became very upset, and put his hands over his ears. He said, "What presumption! I've never heard anything like this! No one can say he is sure he has eternal life, or that he is going to heaven. We hope someday in the distant future, after many years in purgatory, by the grace of God, to finally make it to heaven. But not even the pope would make such a presumptuous statement like you, Franz."

I quickly replied, "If the pope cannot say that he is going to heaven if he dies today, then he must not be sure he is saved." I was young, and also a very new Christian, and had had no help with my Christian faith and walk, so I believed that I was the only Christian around. And I had found in the Book of Romans all the assurance I needed that I really was a child of God.

After the priest left that day, my parents and two single aunts were so very upset. The aunts declared, "Franz, you have just lost everything of your inheritance which we have written for you."

Well, I thought, *I could care less; I have the main thing, and that is eternal life.*

Then my father said, "Franz, there is the door! You leave right now, and we don't ever want to see you again. I had three sons.

Two died in the war. My third son died today. There is the door!"

I walked out, extremely sad and deeply disturbed, because I loved my parents very much, even more now that I had become a Christian. I will never forget walking the streets of Duren, which was still being rebuilt, not knowing where to turn or what to do. My heart was broken over the loss of my parents and home. Elisabeth and I were engaged at that time, and I went to see her. Her parents were kind enough to take me in for a few days. They didn't understand what had happened. They couldn't understand my beliefs, but they were kind enough to say, "Franz, we take you in for a few days, until you find another place to stay."

I thought, *Great! But Lord, what do I do next?*

Then I remembered the letter I had just received from Dr. McFarlane, in which he told of visiting British prisoner-of-war camps. There was a German prisoner, recently released, whose name was Willie Blech, who had become a believer there in the English camp. He had written, "Franz, please visit him in Essen at this address."

Here is one lead, I thought. *I will go to Essen.* Essen is about a hundred miles away from my Duren. I took the train, not knowing what a wonderful experience was waiting for me in Essen.

Willie was the first Christian brother I had ever met, and we talked all night together. Then his landlady had another bed free, so I stayed on there. Willie and I started a Bible study, which later grew into a church. When Elisabeth and I married, Essen became our hometown for five years!

13 Elisabeth

Elisabeth has been my beloved wife for almost forty years now. I was twenty-two and playing the guitar in a dance band in my hometown when she came to a Saturday night dance where I was performing. I fell in love with her as soon as I saw her and said to my friends, "That is the girl I'm going to marry!"

As we got to know each other we found we had the same interests, especially in music. We enjoyed doing many things together. We were engaged and planned to marry. When I became a believer and started spending so much time reading the Bible, of course I wanted her to be as excited as I was about the truth I had found, and wanted her to believe too. It was hard for me to realize that not everyone would immediately grasp the excitement of this truth, and immediately accept the "good news" of the gospel.

After each week of work in Dusseldorf, I would spend the weekend at Elisabeth's home. I would talk with her and give her portions of the Bible to study and meditate upon, and then say that we would talk about it the following week. In my eagerness I bombarded her too aggressively. Today I really can't understand how she put up with me at that time! I had so changed from the person she had known.

As time went on I realized that nothing was happening; she was not accepting what I was trying to force on her.

One day I read in 2 Corinthians 6:14, "Do not be unequally yoked together with unbelievers. For what fellowship has righteousness with lawlessness? And what communion has light with darkness?" All of a sudden I realized, *I can't marry Elisabeth! How could we go through life together, pulling in different directions? How could we build a marriage if we were unequally yoked together?* I knew that I had to break the relationship. I loved Elisabeth so very, very much, yet the Bible was so clear.

I was miserable as the weekend came closer. I prayed a lot. "Lord, give me courage for what has to be done." I will never forget that Saturday when I said, "Elisabeth, I have to talk to you." We went to a back room to be alone, as I wanted to get it over with quickly.

But Elisabeth spoke first; she said, "Franz, I have to tell you something I am excited about, that happened Wednesday. You know, Franz, you kept trying to force me to read Scripture, but I didn't want to. Yet, I kept reading the sixth chapter of John over and over again. And, you know what? On Wednesday I really felt this was true, and I asked the Lord Jesus to change my life. I believed, on Wednesday!"

I could scarcely believe what I was hearing. I was rejoicing inside and thinking how good the Lord is. At that time I didn't tell her what I had come prepared to say. Months later I told her the story.

On June 4, 1954, we were married, and I can only quote from Psalm 106: "The Lord is good. His mercy endures forever"!

I can tell you after almost forty years of marriage that we have experienced something we never thought possible: a loving relationship between husband and wife that continues to grow each day. To have one another through the years, and now with the children grown up to have more time to pray with one another and have devotions together day by day, is a wonderful experience. I thank God for marriage, and I praise God for Elisabeth.

14 <u>*Off to America*</u>

As I have told you, I played and studied a lot of music—chamber music as well as jazz. However there was an increasing problem with my left wrist, which often made it necessary to stop in the middle of playing. There was a painful inflammation, and after months of going to doctors and trying medicines and treatments and finding that nothing helped, I came to the painful decision that I should give up pursuing an active music career and try something else. It seemed that my world had broken apart; I thought I could never live without music. However by faith I believed that John 10:10, where Jesus says, "I have come that they might have life, and that they might have it more abundantly" or, "have a full and meaningful life," meant that God had something special in store for me.

At that point I visited my parents' home again. As time went on my parents had found out where I was in Essen. They had come to the place of forgiving me, and had even begun to read the Bible themselves. When I visited we studied the Bible together, and they did come to understand that salvation was through the death of Jesus for them, and that they could have the assurance of heaven. They never did leave the Catholic Church, but the important thing is that we will be together in heaven.

Shortly after being reconciled with my parents, I found an advertisement in the newspaper which said that Ibach, a renowned old German piano manufacturing company, was looking for apprentices. *Piano making would still have a lot to do with music*, I thought. They took me on at the Ibach factory when I was about twenty-three years old. I loved working with my hands, and heard much music too. It was fascinating to go through all the phases of building pianos. Finally I learned tuning and tone regulating. I worked in that factory for five years, then found another advertisement which led me to becoming a concert technician for a concert agency in Dusseldorf. I did a lot of the tuning of concert pianos, and also was able to go to many concerts with Elisabeth. Then as now, most of the pianos used for concerts were Steinways, and as a piano technician I fell in love with the Steinway.

The years in Essen were happy ones. We lived in a nice area called Ruttenscheid. Because of my tuning the pianos for them, we attended many concerts—in Essen, Dusseldorf, and Cologne. We also were active in the Baptist Church, and had Bible studies in our home. Then in 1959 our first son, Peter, was born. We were now a real family!

One day we read in a weekly publication of the Baptist Church an advertisement which stated that, "If anyone wants to come to America or to New York City, the German Emanuel Baptist Church of New York City would be happy to extend a helping hand." The name given to write to was Assaf Husman, a pastor in Woodside, New York. A few days later, Elisabeth said, "Franz, just for fun, why don't you write to that pastor, and see how life is for a piano tuner in America!"

Well, I wrote—"just for fun." I said, "Dear Pastor: I am a piano technician and I tune for concerts and recording sessions. What possibility would there be for me to work in New York?"

A couple of weeks later I got this reply: "Please come. Everything is ready for you. Please come. I contacted Steinway. I told them about you, and Steinway would be very interested for you to come and work with them. We also have a three-room apartment ready for you when you come. Please, can you come?"

I was immediately enthusiastic, and said, "Let's go."

But Elisabeth was not so sure. Peter was just two-and-a-half years old and she was pregnant with our second child. After much prayer and soul-searching we decided to go to America. It became clearer and clearer to us that the Lord was leading the way. With Peter we went to the American embassy in Frankfurt to apply for a visa. The vice-consul who interviewed us at the American Embassy was a very friendly young man. When he heard that I was a piano tuner and that I was going to work for Steinway, he jokingly said, "Oh, do we need tuners! The whole country is out of tune. You'd better come."

In just a couple of hours we had our visas. However we made arrangements not to leave Germany before September, as we wanted our second child to be born in Germany.

Our parents were sad to see us go, especially my parents, as they had lost two sons in the war and I was the only one left. But we promised them we would come home on vacation every year, and that seemed acceptable to them. We kept that promise as long as my parents lived.

Michael was born on June 14, 1962, and the following September we sailed from Hamburg on the Hanseatic. En route to America the ship docked in Southampton, England, for a few hours, where we had a wonderful surprise! We had written to our friend Dr. McFarlane, in Cardiff, that God seemed to be leading us to America, and that our ship would leave Hamburg September 21st. We did not know that he had found out what time our ship would make its five-hour stop in Southampton. He came on board to meet us. It had been quite a few years since my earlier encounter with him, which really had been a turning point in my life; but he was still a wonderfully friendly gentleman, full of the love of the Lord.

Dr. McFarlane had one main concern as he talked with us: "Franz, Elisabeth, what is driving you to America? Is it just the desire of adventure?"

We explained how it had come about, and that we were sure God was leading us. He was happy about that, but he asked us to write him as soon as we got to New York. We had a wonderful time right on that promenade deck, and at the end we huddled together praying for each other. We were never to see each other again; shortly after we arrived in New York, Dr. McFarlane passed from this life into the presence of his beloved Lord.

We arrived in New York on September 26. Pastor Husman himself came to pick us up at the pier. His Pontiac station wagon was huge, yet I wondered how he could find room for all our things. But it worked out fine . . . with all eleven suitcases, plus Peter and Michael and the baby carriage. He then drove us to the German church, at 61-10 Thirty-first Avenue in Woodside; the church gave us an apartment, furnished and well-stocked with food, for our first few days in America.

I will never forget going to Steinway for the first time the next morning. I met Henry, John, and Frederick Steinway. After we got acquainted, we all went out together for lunch. They invited all the German men who were working in the Steinway office to come along. I was so proud of the papers I had—my degrees in piano technology, which meant so much in Europe. I had had them translated into English, which had cost quite a lot, and was surprised that the Steinways simply glanced at them and said, "Well, Franz, that's all very nice, but you just start working and we will see what you can do." I immediately liked the easygoing way of the Americans, being called by my first name and encouraged to call everyone else by their first name. This would have been impossible in Germany. There everything was so formal, even if people worked all their lives in the same office.

There were other things about New York that were hard to take. I remember the fumes and the dirt in the streets. Walking home from the subway one of those first days I saw a big, fat rat behind a gas station. And when I got home Elisabeth was sitting on the kitchen table with her legs up, looking scared.

"What's the matter?" I asked.

"There's a big animal in the bathroom," she said.

There was a huge cockroach in the bathtub, trying to climb out and always skidding back down. Then at the first prayer meeting we went to, we saw a big water bug running back and forth behind the pulpit and trying to climb down the steps, while no one seemed to notice. Then on the first Sunday we went out for a stroll, as we used to do in Germany after church. Looking from the window we saw trees, and thought it was a park. We took the kids with us, holding Peter's hand and pushing Michael's carriage. It turned out to be a cemetery; still, we were happy to be under trees, and we walked a bit. But soon the caretaker came and told us the cemetery was closing and we would have to leave! Yes, it was very different from the life we were used to.

The church was like a big family, and the people included us in many things they were doing; but soon we realized we should move to an apartment of our own, as the apartment we were in was really meant for missionaries. As we looked for apartments, they all seemed too expensive. Some places were dirty and run-down; other nicer places would not take children. Finally we found an apartment where we could live rent-free by being the superintendents. We had to collect the rent and keep the building clean and do some repair. Although we made some mistakes, the landlord always said, "You are honest people and you take good care of collecting the rent, so I am happy to have you."

After a few years we had enough money to begin buying a house in Lynnbrook, a forty-minute ride from New York City on the Long Island train. We now had a car and could do things like go upstate for picnics. Finally we were very happy and felt at home in America. It seemed that the Lord had wonderfully led and cared for us. We do not always have things easy, but I think often about Psalm 23: "The LORD is my shepherd, I shall not want. . . . He leads me beside the still waters. . . . He leads me in the paths of righteousness for his name's sake." Or of Psalm 57: "Delight yourself in the LORD and he will direct your paths." Or Matthew 6:33: "Seek ye first the kingdom of God and his righteousness, and all these things will be added unto you." (KJV)

I continue to be very much involved in my work at Steinway. Our children are all happily married. Dear Peter has our first grandchild. Both Peter and Michael are involved in working with pianos. I never pushed this kind of work on them. It just grew. In fact I would say they are "piano nuts"! Both went to work for Steinway immediately after high school. We wanted them to go to college but they wanted to work with pianos. They got their college education while working at Steinway and going to Nassau Community College in the evenings.

Peter is now with Falcone Piano Manufacturing Company, which is reviving the old American Mason and Hamlin piano, which was a marvelously designed instrument forty or fifty years ago. It is good for Steinway to have a genuine competitor. Michael, as I have mentioned, has a leading position in Steinway. Dear Ellen graduated from college, and is now married, making her career at present with Lufthansa Airlines.

For me it is a wonderful combination to be able to be creative and working with music, and to go on in life with the assurance that Jesus is my Savior and Lord. One time I was talking with a great artist about my excitement in living with my Bible, and he said suddenly, "Franz, are you telling me that there is something greater in life than music?" And I said, "Yes, there is something greater in life than music: It is knowing the living God, and coming to him in the way he has opened to us." I talked with him about sin, and explained that, although it is great to enjoy the arts and music, yet we also have to deal with the sin in our lives.

Recently I met a woman professor from the music department of the Jerusalem University who was on a speaking tour in the States. We talked about Horowitz. She suddenly said she could hardly wait to get back to Jerusalem and her beloved Israel. I then told her that I am a Bible-believing man, and that I love Israel very much. I said, "As a Jewish person, you probably will not agree with me, but I am sure that Jesus is the Jewish Messiah."

To my amazement she immediately interrupted me and said, "I never talk much about it, but you must know it can't be anyone else. If only my people the Jews would trouble themselves enough to read the Old Testament, they would see for themselves that it can't be anyone else but Jesus."

I was so excited to hear that from a Jewish person. Then she went on and said, "No one but Jesus fulfills all the prophecy in the Old Testament concerning the Messiah."

How right she was. I once studied, for months and months,

all the Old Testament prophecies concerning the Messiah; I
found more than three hundred. Think for a moment about just
one of those three hundred prophecies—one concerning his
birthplace. In Micah 5:2 we read,

But you, Bethlehem Ephrathah,
Though you are little among the thousands of Judah,
Yet out of you shall come forth to Me
The One to be Ruler in Israel,
Whose goings forth are from of old,
From everlasting.

The Israeli ambassador to the United Nations, Chaim Herzog
(who is now President in Israel), lived with his family right on
Fifth Avenue. I was his piano tuner. One time when I had just
tuned his piano he kindly said he was very glad to meet me. I
told him that as a Christian I pray for the peace of Jerusalem,
according to Psalm 122:6: "Pray for the peace of Jerusalem, may
they prosper who love you." He became very excited and said,
"Mr. Mohr, when you and your family come to Israel, we will do
something very special for you."

Never did I think that, in coming to the United States, I would
develop such deep friendships with Jewish people, especially
Jewish artists. I thought that, being German, I had better shut
up and say nothing about my faith, because of all that Nazi
Germany did to the Jews.

One beautiful, clear, cold November day I was looking forward to spending a few days with Rudolf Serkin at his home in
Vermont, to work on his pianos. I have been there many times.
It is a farm on the top of a mountain, which he bought many
years ago; he made the most beautiful studio, done in knotty
pine, with a huge window overlooking the mountains, with no
house in sight. I love to go there simply to get away from the
hustle and bustle of New York City.

I was planning to stop, on the way there, to meet the parents
of Gary, our daughter Ellen's fiance at that time; we were going
to have dinner together. I left right after church, and had a great

time driving there. I was close to my exit when, because of some frozen spots on the highway I lost control of the car. I never did realize what all happened. I remember seeing rocks in front of me, and wishing the car would stop rocking around! People who were watching later told me that the car flipped over and rolled at least three times and finally came to a stop standing on its wheels! I saw a lady running toward me, and tried to open the window to talk to her, but found there was no window, and that the roof had caved in to the seat next to me . . . and yet I still had my glasses hanging on my chest!

A young man ran toward me and said, "You must be a Christian."

"Why?"

"Because you were praising the Lord."

I was not conscious that I had said anything.

Rather than meeting in a nice restaurant that day, we were all meeting in the Brattleboro hospital! That night the doctor said to me, "You had your seat belt on across your chest, and all the little blood vessels are burst and they will give you some trouble, but there is nothing broken." I had trouble sleeping that night, and though I had called Elisabeth and the people at Avis Rent-a-Car, I still was in a state of shock. The next morning I called my good friend Edith Schaeffer, and as I told her what had happened she said, "Let me read you the *Daily Light* portions for today, Franz." *Daily Light* is a publication consisting of portions of Scripture linked together. The Word of God went deep into my spirit as Edith read it to me:

> Lord, thou hast been our dwelling place in all generations. He that dwelleth in the secret place of the most high shall abide under the shadow of the Almighty. I will say to the Lord: He is my refuge and fortress. Your life is hid with Christ in God. He that touches you touches the apple of his eye. Fear not. Stand still and see the salvation of the Lord. God is our refuge and strength, a very present help in time of trouble. Therefore we will not fear. Jesus spoke unto them saying, "Be of good cheer, it is I, be not afraid. Why are you troubled? And why do you think such things in your heart? Behold my hands and my

feet, that it is I myself, handle me and see, for a spirit has not flesh and bones as you see me have." I know whom I have believed and am persuaded that he is able to keep that which I have committed unto him against that day.

I secured my own copy of that very special reading from *Daily Light*, and have kept it with me ever since that day. We go through life with all kinds of afflictions and hardships, but God is with us.

PART 4

The
Technician
at Work

by Edith Schaeffer

15 *An Afternoon of On-Stage Tuning*

It is a windy, chilly day in October, and as the taxi starts and stops its way in jerks through the noontime traffic, I watch the faces of people hurrying, running, walking slowly, dragging themselves, and even jogging down the streets. How could faces differ so strikingly (forgetting shades of skin color) when everyone has two ears, a nose, eyes, and a chin? What unlocks a personality, or pulls off the covering of ideas, attitudes, longings, aspirations that are in the minds of these strolling or jostling or hurrying people?

I am already counting out my money as the taxi comes to an abrupt stop at Carnegie Hall. "Around the corner, please, at the stage door."

As I go under the scaffolding and through the stage entrance door, Franz is there with his welcoming smile. "Let's go over to the Carnegie Deli and have some matzo ball soup before we begin the afternoon's work."

I heartily agree to that, but there is a discouragingly long line in front of, down the sidewalk, and around the corner from the deli as many other people with the same idea were waiting to get in. As this is an appointment with a piano, there is no time to "queue up," so we settle for a Greek Restaurant near Carnegie and have a satisfying Greek chicken soup—good for colds as well as for a cold day.

Franz wants to tell me the schedule for the afternoon in preparation for the concert with Horacio Gutierrez and the

Pittsburgh Symphony Orchestra. There is to be the tuning, voicing, and regulating of the piano for a rehearsal later in the afternoon. Then the piano will need a bit of "touching up" after the rehearsal, to be sure that everything will be exactly right for the concert. Franz's wife Elisabeth, along with his daughter Ellen and her husband Gary, his son Michael and his wife Donna are to meet us for supper at the Chinese restaurant before the evening concert. Franz, of course, will be sitting out of sight at the right of the stage for the concert. I will be with Elisabeth, as the tickets are not all together.

After settling these routine details, Franz's eyes light up with enthusiasm as he tells me that the piano Gutierrez is going to play is none other than the Horowitz piano—the one you have been reading so much about. Franz is eager to have the piano ready to do its best under Gutierrez's skillful fingers. Gutierrez's great playing is very familiar to Franz, and he has prepared pianos for him before; but preparing this familiar piano for a different artist, and putting the two together, seems to fire Franz with an eagerness to get going—something like a race horse pulling ahead a bit before the signal.

The soup and a roll and coffee take time enough. There is no time for any more. "Okay," Franz says, "Let's go!"

The tall guard of the stage entrance greets Franz with a smile and takes his key out to open the door to the stairway leading up to the labyrinth of doors and halls. Then come more stairs and sharp corners, dressing rooms, practice rooms, the conductor's room, rooms with arrays of equipment, a bewildering maze one needs a guide to get through. But Franz knows his way, and on we go until we arrive backstage where there is a jungle of con-trols—wires, switches, a high desk, boxes that look strong and secure, of different sizes.

"Watch the wire! Step carefully!"

The Orchestra Manager nods at us. "Hi," he says, and turning to Franz remarks, "Sorry for the noise."

We walk across the stage to the piano. "Here it is," says Franz, lovingly, "this wonderful piano that has travelled so many places with us." He hits a note or two, pulls out the stool, opens his tool case and arranges the tools, listens a moment and then walks back across the stage to the Carnegie Hall manager and talks with him a moment.

The result of that little conversation is that the manager asks the man vacuuming the rugs up and down the aisles to please stop. "Turn off the vacuum, the 'pitch' is mixing with the piano, and it is impossible for Franz to hear correctly."

Someone has brought me a chair by this time, and I sit down on the audience side of the piano, looking out at the vast empty hall, as the now silent vacuum cleaner is rolled away only to make way for a very different sound.

Is this "quiet"? I think to myself as stagehands begin putting up a graduated set of platforms. *Put* up? I should say *bang* up. Lift, drop in place, bang, shove, scrape. Carts are wheeled noisily across the stage with more pieces while voices call out orders of one sort or another. Suddenly a section of the stage floor sinks down like an elevator without sides, and several men disappear, only to reappear with more pieces to complete the tiered platform.

Franz seems oblivious to the assorted noises. You see, it was the "pitch" of the vacuum cleaner which made it impossible for his ears to distinguish the tones and sounds he needed to hear as he bong-bong-bonged away at the piano, over and over again, moving from one precise piece of perfection to another and another. No, Franz isn't bothered by these other sounds.

Ohhhhhh . . . here come mysterious shapes, wrapped up for travel. They are the kettle drums. And the next shape is unwrapped to reveal the cymbals. The men are working more quickly now—snap, bang, push. The music stands are being unfolded and put in place, with chairs being unfolded and placed exactly where each musician will need to have one.

My eyes turn to the empty Carnegie Hall, with its red velvet seats in hushed rows, awaiting the music lovers' arrival, but seeming to look now at the empty chairs on the stage, the silent drums, and the skilled men moving rapidly to transform the stage. These efficient stagehands are middle-aged with thinning hair; young with thick, curly hair; tall, slim, short, heavy, strong, competent, and, as Franz once remarked, "Well paid! They are very well paid!"

Now the stagehands have come to move the piano into position for Horacio Gutierrez.

"Okay?"

Franz, already dressed in his dark suit for the evening, jumps up smilingly and helps push the piano across the stage into its place at the front.

The precious piano which Wanda and Vladimir Horowitz had received as a wedding present is now taking its place on the stage so familiar to it, but starting a new chapter of life. If only the piano could talk, it could tell of the voyage to Moscow and Japan, and of so much more. It would tell of the cheers and clapping in this very hall as Horowitz played the final note in one concert after another. *But, I muse to myself, the piano must be happy in its own way to have Franz working on it again, to put it in its best condition.* As Franz continues to give it the right color and voice, I feel sure it is looking forward to being able to "sing" again.

And if the walls of Carnegie could speak, or whisper, what fabulous stories they could exchange with the pianos. If the walls—the vaulted ceilings, every curve of the four-tiered balconies, the columns and the gold-leaf fine work on the acoustically well-prepared curve at the front of the stage—could talk: There are one hundred years of stories to tell of amazingly different artists, instruments, performances. History has been woven in the sound of music and the growth of genius within these walls.

A shiver of expectation for the evening's music goes up my spine as I realize I'm getting a glimpse of a part of this very busy hundredth-year celebration of Carnegie Hall. So many times Steinway pianos will be prepared for so many concerts, yet right now I'm sitting, like a mouse under the Queen's chair, among the empty chairs of the orchestra, realizing that the stagehands are now finished, and that Franz is also finished and trying out the piano, first with a series of chords, then with some hymns, listening for any slight flaw.

Voices burst in, and this time it is the orchestra coming in with their instruments, ready for the rehearsal. My place will soon be down in the empty hall, listening to the rehearsal, taking a few more notes in my notebook, and feasting on the music I will be privileged to hear.

Now in comes Horacio Gutierrez and his wife, Pat, warmly greeting Franz and myself. Franz has tuned for Horacio many times and knows him well, appreciating his playing so very much. Horacio has played as soloist with many orchestras and you may be hearing his records, as well as hearing him in concert in your own city. Horacio adjusts his stool, sits down, and a burst of music, a sudden waterfall of crystal notes fills the hall. Some notes are coming from the brass section, a cello is doing something else. Glorious chaos as the music of the evening is being promised.

"Let's go out for a bite to eat, and get back in time for the rehearsal," says Franz. "Horacio is satisfied with the piano as it is, and I won't touch it again until after he rehearses."

We stop to greet the first cellist of the Pittsburgh orchestra, a lovely, vivid young woman, and hurry off to go through all the halls and stairways again, passing all shapes and sizes of musicians and instruments.

Later, we settle down in our seats in the empty hall with only a few scattered people there for the rehearsal. Franz will listen with different ears, loving and enjoying the music but also listening to pick up any hint of a need for him to adjust something before the evening concert.

I lose myself in watching and listening as the Rachmaninoff concerto flows downstream and splashes against cliffs into quiet pools between ferns and moss. How fantastically music can communicate, without any language problem! Intensity is communicated without words, felt in one's intellect as well as with one's ears: intensity on the part of Horacio's fingers, flying over the keys precisely, flawlessly; intensity on the part of the orchestra members as they move between strict attention to the conductor's directing, replaying certain parts, blending in their instruments carefully with the soloist's piano.

How long ago, I think to myself, *were they conservatory students dreaming of being in Carnegie some day . . . and this is it!* Tonight the hall is to be packed. This is the last rehearsal.

My thoughts shift to the flow of notes. Is this like *breathing* for the artist? Or is every note in his mind before it comes forth? What about the blend—of piano, flute, violin, cello, viola, harp? The physical work of fingers, shoulders, necks, heads, backs, feet on pedals, the conductor's arms, back, head, legs. The physical coordination of the whole orchestra has to be there to give the soloist his proper place. Which of the people involved needs the greatest discipline of mind and body, the most precise movement of fingers?

The excitement of the whole, felt in the conductor's movements as well as in the sound, is an excitement similar to watching lightening streak the sky with zigzag movement while a moon remains visible and ocean waves leap higher and higher.

What stunning enjoyment can be provided by human creativity at its best, and what stunning satisfaction there is in knowing that the wonders of the universe were created by the Creator who is infinite and unlimited, and who created man and woman in his own image, to be able to be creative in such diverse ways. Human beings, finite and limited, but with myriad ideas and capabilities to make instruments, compositions, and halls in which to perform, and to have the talent to perform. The Creator makes human beings with ears to hear, eyes to see, and intellects to think and appreciate the communication of other minds.

With this "world view," the satisfaction of music resounding from one's ribs as well as ears and mind, is a satisfaction that turns into true worship of the Creator who made it all possible.

During the break between the first and second halves of the rehearsal—the second half will be Tchaikovsky's Symphony No. 3—Franz and I talk with Sid Kaplan, Manager of the Pittsburgh Orchestra, about Carnegie Hall before and after the renovation. It is amazing how acoustics can be affected by very small things. Mr. Kaplan tells us about a hall in which a six-inch curtain across the top of the stage, just below the ceiling, was cutting the sound. The sound was being trapped by that one little curtain, spoiling the purity of the notes, even though the instruments and the performers were doing well.

As Kaplan talks and explains all this, I think about the "symphony of history," in which we are all "instruments." Are we out of tune? Is the problem one of not following the Conductor? Have we rehearsed and gotten the "kinks" out? I think of Moses leading Israel out of Egypt, and how, as Moses was up on Sinai getting instructions from the Conductor, his followers were prancing around the golden calf.

How different history would have been if certain people had played their notes faithfully, instead of walking off the stage. Who is adding to the chaos and discord of this portion of history by not following the Conductor? Who is a part of the "six-inch curtain" cutting the acoustics, blurring the sound? Who is adding to the confusion of uncertainty as to what the music is meant to be communicating? It would be too bad if the hundredth-year celebration of Carnegie Hall were to be spoiled in any way, but it is a much more serious thing to be contributing to the spoiling of the symphony meant to demonstrate the existence of the Creator. What a tragic, devastating sabotage if we diminish the clarity and beauty of the Master Composer's composition.

We are chased out of the second half of the rehearsal, as the conductor wants to be alone with his orchestra. I sit on the stairway steps, which so soon will be full of feet—feet in high heeled shoes, in men's oxfords; big, little, taking measured steps or running up the stairs; voices above the feet speaking many languages, sounding like a railroad station as New Yorkers and out-of-towners babble away. I sit writing notes while talking with the lovely eight-year-old daughter of a cellist as she waits for her father's rehearsal to end. Soon it is time for me to meet Franz, Elisabeth, and the family for our meal, before becoming a part of the evening audience.

The evening concert is a thrilling combination of Horacio Gutierrez's skill, wonderful touch, and acute sensitivity to the music flowing through him, as well as through the well-prepared piano—which has its own memories of being played by Horowitz! The flow of the orchestra with the piano brings forth a completeness that is exciting as it fills each one there to his or her personal capacity to respond and enjoy. The Tchaikovsky is really a great second half to the evening. How satisfying sound can be if each note is where it should be!

Going up to the Green Room afterwards, it is very special to be able to express appreciation to the artist, Horacio Gutierrez, but even more special to be there as Franz receives a hug from the artist as he thanks him for the wonderful way he has prepared the piano. "What a wonderful piano, and what a privilege to play on it after all these years of Horowitz's playing on it . . . and your caring for the tuning, tone control, and all the rest. Thank you, Franz."

Yes, we each make a difference, whether we are doing a negative thing like that six-inch curtain, or a positive thing like making sure that the notes will be in tune.

16 *Jahja Ling*

It was Saturday, November 10th, 1991. Bob and Evelyn Baldwin had taken my sister Elsa and me to Cleveland's Severance Hall for the opening concert of the Cleveland Orchestra's new season—for our birthday treat. Jahja Ling, who was then resident conductor of the Cleveland Orchestra, was conducting, and as Elsa and I were born in China, it seemed appropriate to be watching this very fine conductor born in Indonesia of Chinese parents—but of course not as many years ago! We settled down for our treat, anticipating the wonderful music of this great orchestra, as well as the joy of watching our friend Jahja conduct.

Jahja is an exceptionally exciting conductor to watch, with his vivid, lively movements, not a copy of any other conductor, but an original choreographer of his own dance movements—his body swaying, hands moving like flowing liquid with untaught freedom of form, very like a smoothly gliding bird. Then, suddenly the dance becomes fiery with rapid, forceful arm and hand movements playing on the whole orchestra as if on a giant organ. Both feet suddenly are off the floor, the tails of his black formal jacket flying as he leads Tchaikovsky's symphony to its crashing end. The sound crashes into the audience's ears with thrilling waves of sound, with everyone as involved as rocks at the shore in a high storm, when sound as well as water flows into every crevice, washing equally over rocks and pebbles. The audience responds with a thunderous clapping that asks for more and more curtain calls, and continues with a standing ovation.

Our minds now need to jump back some years, to the time of

Jahja Ling's birth in 1951 in Jakarta, Indonesia, of Chinese parents who taught their children to place incense before household idols in their rituals of ancestor worship. Jahja's father was also an educated official of the city, and wanted his son to begin his education early. A mainland Chinese kindergarten teacher was brought into the home to begin a kindergarten for Jahja's sake, and other children were brought in to study with him. The teacher played little children's songs on the fine piano as part of the daily singing lessons. One day a substitute teacher taught, saying she could not play the piano so they would have to wait for the regular teacher to be well again. While the children were clamoring for a song, four-year-old Jahja climbed up on the piano stool and played a piece without missing a note!

It was soon found that he could play whatever he watched the teacher play. The discovery of his musical genius caused his father to immediately start him studying with a piano teacher. By the time Jahja was seventeen he had won the Jakarta piano competition and a year later was awarded the Rockefeller grant to attend the Juilliard School in New York. A long list of honors follow.

Although Jahja Ling was brought up in an atmosphere of ancestor worship, his Chinese kindergarten teacher was a Christian, and took him to her Sunday school for "more education." Jahja's mother went to Sunday school with him, and became thrilled with her own gradual understanding of truth. They were both Christians as she made a home for her son in a New York City apartment when he was at Juilliard. And while in New York Jahja met another music student, Jane, also a Chinese Christian, whom he married. Today he conducts the Florida Orchestra, as well as serving as guest conductor for orchestras all over the world.

What, you may ask, has this to do with Franz Mohr? Read on! Jahja, as a really brilliant pianist, was looking and praying for a truly good piano, and kept his eyes out for one on sale for a good price. While in Los Angeles helping with the music for one of Stephan Tong's evangelistic crusades (Stephan is a Chinese evangelist from Jakarta), Jahja kept looking at ads for

secondhand pianos in the *Los Angeles Times*. He found one for
$14,500, but after calling his wife and talking it over decided
that they could not pay a dollar more than $13,000, and he came
home without one. Later he was conducting in Washington, and
looked at a Steinway in good condition for $30,000. It was
tempting! "But no, it is too much." He considered borrowing
the money, but decided against it.

Back in Cleveland, Jahja found that a concert Steinway had
been pushed into his office. "What piano is this?" he asked.
"Oh," came the reply, "this is one we are going to auction maybe;
anyway, we will sell it to some very special person who would
really love it and use it. It's the one George Szell bought for
Cleveland in 1967."

"What," asked Jahja, "would you ask for it?"

"That depends. That depends on who wants it. Now if *you*
want to buy it, Jahja, you can have it for $10,000."

Jahja thought to himself, "If this could be rebuilt, it would be
absolutely wonderful. However, I could be happy with it simply
tuned and regulated locally." So he took it, and there it stood
in a perfect spot in his living room, a shiny, polished
mahogany—CD 15, the concert grand Steinway, looking marvelous against white walls, one of which had a fantastic calligra-
phy in Chinese characters painted in black with wonderful free
brush strokes, a work of art, which if you don't know Mandarin
you can't read, but which if you do is a striking verse from
Scripture. The artist was none other than Stephan Tong, who
had stood on a ladder painting his gift to the Ling family!

Four months later, Rudolf Serkin (then eighty-five) came to
play the solo piano portion of Beethoven's **Fifth, the**
"Emperor" Concerto. Serkin had played in Chicago on
Wednesday, and this Cleveland Orchestra concert was on
Sunday. He had been ill and resting in bed in a hotel in between
concerts, and those in the orchestra who knew and loved him
were worried that he might not be able to play this vigorous
piece. Before the concert, Cleveland's Concert Master, Daniel
Majeske, said to Marilyn, his wife, Steve, his son (also a violinist
in the orchestra), and me, "Do pray for Rudy Serkin as he plays;

he really isn't well. You know, he has done so much for me in the past; I want to help him all I can tonight."

Daniel had studied with Serkin in Curtis Music Institute in Philadelphia, and at Marlboro, Serkin's summer music festival and school in Vermont. "He really cared for his students, and always was such an inspiration to keep practicing, no matter how much we felt we knew something; yet he was always gracious. We are all praying he will do well with that long piece tonight. It needs so much strength."

Franz Mohr had been in Chicago to tune for Serkin on Wednesday, then had flown back to New York to go with Elisabeth to what was to be Horowitz's last birthday party, and then back to Cleveland for Serkin's concert. As we stood together in that maze of halls backstage of Severance Hall, Jahja came over to Franz, who was telling about Horowitz's party. Franz had tuned and voiced Serkin's piano (brought from Vermont, but by way of Chicago!) and now turned to say hello to Jahja. "Franz," said Jahja, "do you know what? I bought the CD 15!"

"Wow!" exclaimed Franz, "*You* got *that* piano? I love that piano. You know, I remember the day George Szell heard Firkusny play that piano in Lincoln Center and then chose it definitely for Cleveland. I have a deep affection for that piano. It has a special voice."

Then Franz asked a little anxiously, "Is it in good condition?"

Jahja made a little movement of his head and shrugged his shoulder just a bit, "Well, it needs more work, I think."

Franz replied to that with a firm, "I would like to restore it—to put in all new felt and completely new action and new hammers."

When they both had a free week, Franz went through the Steinway factory with his son Michael to choose the right hammers and other parts for CD 15. (Michael, who works in the factory, had been on the lookout for just the right parts.) Then Franz came and lived in the Ling home for a week, while he worked on the piano. Franz really enjoyed that week, and the Lings enjoyed him. Ling's mother cooked special Indonesian meals for Franz, and they exchanged stories of their personal histories. Franz spoke in the Chinese church on the Sunday he was there.

How exciting history is when it is possible to follow pianos and people through their lives! Here was the little boy from an ancestor worshiping home in Jakarta, and the teenager so filled with hate during the bombings in Germany. Now, far from Jakarta, far from Germany, they were praying together to the same God, the God of Abraham, Isaac, and Jacob; the Father, Son, and Holy Ghost whom they both loved. And they had been brought together by a *piano* they both deeply appreciate, respecting the fact of history that before Szell chose it for Cleveland, Arturo Benedetti Michelangeli had played it in Carnegie Hall, and had practiced on it until the very last minute. Only beings with real minds and intellects—that is, *human* beings, who have personality and are are not machines—can be in such awe of history.

As for Serkin's evening with the Cleveland Orchestra, it was a superb concert! When it was over, everyone in the orchestra had tears in their eyes. It was magnificent and overwhelming and powerful. Where did the strength come from? Serkin looked so frail as he walked in, so frail as he sat there waiting for the precise moment to hit the first chords.

Frail? He played with an unbelievable power and strength. It was his genius, his skill, his beauty of interpretation; yes, it was Serkin at his best. But I do believe that, as we truly prayed for him, God answered in the words of Isaiah 40:29-31: "He giveth power to the faint; and to them that have no might he increaseth strength. Even the youths shall faint and be weary, and the young men shall utterly fall: But they that wait upon the LORD shall renew their strength; they shall mount up with wings as eagles; they shall run, and not be weary; and they shall walk, and not faint."

That night Rudolf Serkin's fingers were truly renewed with strength; his fingers ran over the keys, walked at times without fainting; but seemed to fly over the keys with "eagles' wings," until the very last notes. "My strength is made perfect in weakness," we are told, as this same holy and everlasting God speaks through Paul.

Who may ask for such strength? Children may ask their father when he has told them to ask. We have been told to pray, "Our Father which art in heaven . . ." We need to become his children, then with trust, as well as love and awe, we may ask for help.

Some time after that November concert, which Jahja had so brilliantly conducted, we were invited to his house to see the piano Franz had so skillfully rebuilt. We met Jahja's boys again, the eleven-year-old now making strides in his piano playing, to the point that his father gives him the privilege of practicing his Chopin on that wonderful CD 15—a rare privilege indeed! We then went to a Chinese restaurant, the Majeske family with their daughters, and other members of the Cleveland orchestra as well as the Baldwins. The conversation centered around music, instruments, concert schedules, conductors, musicians, orchestras, and future hopes and dreams. But also there were discussions of present-day issues and basic worldviews.

The food had to be tasted, smelled, gazed upon, and appreciated, however, and that took attention. Just as music must not be just "background," or it can never be truly listened to and appreciated, so food so wonderfully prepared with the art of cooking, cannot be just "gobbled" or eaten, without taking the time to taste and discover.

Jahja had ordered this feast ahead of time, and a feast it truly was. Indeed it was a symphony of food, not merely one song! He called in the chef and his wife—though we were told that the wife was the real artist of special dishes—and told them verbally how special their dinner had been. Then we all applauded them, just as we had applauded the music, and musicians, and the conductor, and the people behind the scenes—the instrument makers, the composers, and the technicians and tuners.
Bravo! Bravo for the weaving of individual skills and lives into a whole. Bravo for all who have had ideas, made choices, and

worked hard to carry out their ideas so that other people can see, taste, hear, feel what was hidden before—hidden inside the minds of people who acted, and chose to pay the price of exhaustion, to bring forth into the seen world the ideas that had been in the area of imagination.

One of the best evidences of the Creator is the continued creativity of human beings made in his image: Creativity which continues in spite of the ugliness of mankind; creativity which brings forth beauty throughout all the centuries that have come and gone since the Fall, in the midst of wars and the cruelty of person to person . . . such creativity is impossible to explain, apart from the Creator.

As I write these words, the scene Franz described on that Christmas Eve in Germany just before the war ended—with two opposing soldiers playing their trumpets as if speaking to each other with love—is being repeated as Isaac Stern plays his violin in concert in Israel in the midst of the shrill whistle of scud missiles.

The mere chance worshiped by evolutionists is no adequate explanation.

17 The Making of a Great Concert

The program announced that this concert was, "Celebrating a Decade of the Arts." It went on to say, "Long Island University Presents GALA, Saturday, October 27, 1990, 8:00 P.M. LENINGRAD PHILHARMONIC ORCHESTRA OF THE U.S.S.R. Yuri Temirkanov, Music Director; Mariss Jansons, Associate Conductor; Van Cliburn, Pianist."

It was indeed a gala affair, and because it was a benefit, the center block of 900 seats had cost $500 a ticket, with the rest of the 2000 seats at $150 each! People were coming in steadily to fill up all the seats, with a hum of expectant conversation in an atmosphere of excitement, arranging themselves carefully to read their programs, greet friends, or simply to watch the fashion show of people arriving in their elegant best.

There is something to be said for sackcloth as a sign of humility, or T-shirts to project a casual air. But there are times that need to be honored with the wearing of special garments. One honors the bride and groom at a wedding, the orchestra at a gala concert, the birthday person at a formal dinner . . . or the Lord of lords and King of kings at a worship service. Musicians can play marvelously in their casual clothing during a rehearsal, but there is something about a formally dressed orchestra and a conductor with his formal shirt, white tie, and cummerbund . . . his tails flying in an energetic bit of music . . . that gives an added importance to the whole occasion.

"Dressing for the occasion" is not an indication of personal pride but of thoughtfulness, of caring enough to show respect and honor to the people involved in a special event.

As part of the audience, sitting next to Elisabeth Mohr (Franz of course was backstage, standing by for any possible emergency) I arranged my scarf, whispered, "Happy birthday" to Elisabeth, and proceeded to look at the variety of people finding their places, their elegant clothing redecorating the orchestra hall.

Though sitting quietly, my mind was racing back over the day.

Breakfast had been at the Mohrs' home, and at that early morning hour as Franz and I left for the Tilles Center, our parting words had been about the meeting place for Elisabeth's birthday dinner before the concert. "God willing we'll all meet for dinner, Elisabeth. Yes, six o'clock will be all right . . . everyone knows. We might be a little bit late, but we'll be there."

As we drove along early morning roads on that gray day, Franz told me about the piano Van Cliburn would be playing that evening—CD 79, from Steinway's Concert Department. There is a history to how this came to be the piano for that night. Some years before, when Van Cliburn had a concert in Philadelphia, he had brought his own piano from Fort Worth, Texas, and Franz Mohr had brought CD 79 from the Philadelphia Steinway Concert Department, which he had specially tuned for Van Cliburn ahead of time. On the night of Van Cliburn's arrival in Philadelphia, Franz had to come from Connecticut, where he had been speaking to an alumnae group. Michael (Franz's son) drove him down, arriving about midnight.

When they arrived, Franz found that Van Cliburn was practicing on first one and then the other piano, saying he would choose between them. As the night wore on, and the hours ticked by, Van Cliburn fell in love with piano CD 79, but continued to play on first one and then the other. By morning he had decided, and told Franz and Michael that he had chosen CD 79. After that concert he *bought* it and took it home with him!

Now as we arrived at Tilles Center we parked outside the building, where we would not interfere with the big buses bringing the Leningrad orchestra. We hurried through the chill wind to step inside a warm but empty concert hall, reputed to have fine acoustics and an impressive seating arrangement, but with its modern architecture in no way resembling Carnegie Hall.

And this was a tenth anniversary, not a one hundredth. But all that would not matter come evening, when the now empty hall would suddenly become a full house of diverse colors and textures, while the sounds of Tchaikovsky would fill the air and our ears.

For now all ears were filled with the repeated sounds of keys being hit with varying pressure, as Franz began working on the piano. Monotonous? Only if you don't understand. Only if you don't realize that these notes must be in perfect tune for Van Cliburn's masterful fingers to race over, or to touch delicately, to crash with thundering sound, or to whisper with tender touch.

Yes, the piano must be in perfect tune. And on this particular morning the entire instrument must be re-tuned. For as Franz first tried it out, playing a little bit, and then checking it with his tuning fork, he found the pitch to be 441. As you'll remember from a previous chapter, that means the "concert A" vibrates at 441 cycles per second. Now, Franz knew that the Leningrad Orchestra tunes their instruments to 440 cycles, therefore the piano must be the same. So he began changing the pitch of each key to fit precisely with the orchestra.

He sighed a bit, and said, "It is easier to go from 440 to 441, than to bring it down from 441 to 440. You see, the tendency is for the tone to move up."

As he worked steadily, beginning at the base keys and gradually coming up higher . . . suddenly a string broke with a "PING!" Franz bowed his head on his hand, praying a moment for stability, and for *dependability*—praying that the new string would "settle in" for this evening's important concert. It was now 1:00 P.M., and the rehearsal would begin at 5:00 P.M.

"I'll put it up at first," he said as he bent down to his box of tools and extra strings. "Putting it up higher at first will stretch it, and then I can put it down before it is played this evening."

Then with another sigh, after the new string was in place, he turned from the piano to say unhappily, but with firm certainty, "I will need to stay here now with the piano, to readjust it, to touch it up again before the practice, and between the practice and the concert. It always takes time for a new string to settle in. I need to be here to watch over it and do what may have to be done."

Franz now got up, leaving his coat hanging on the little movable stick on the piano, to go find a telephone. He'd have to call Elisabeth and tell her he couldn't make it to her birthday party. Franz as well as Elisabeth and the rest of the party had been looking forward to the combination of dinner and concert. But concert piano tuners are a lot like doctors—they must always be "on call." If a "patient" needs sudden attention, that must come first. If there is need for an "emergency operation," even a wife's birthday dinner must be postponed. The artist must be able to count on the dependability of every note as he approaches his instrument. Only the expert doctor can know when his patient is in danger, needing a certain kind of transfusion or injection . . . and only the expert piano technician can tell what last minute adjusting or touching up the piano needs.

So off Franz went to find a telephone. I followed along, to take a look at what was going on backstage and in the halls. Russian musicians were standing in groups, talking, smoking, leaning against walls looking at their watches . . . watching their instruments being unloaded and their wardrobe trunks being opened up (on end, of course, as one side is for hanging pants and coats and raincoats, and the other side for drawers and shoe racks.) Names are sewn in the backs of jackets and pasted on drawers.

Orchestras on tour . . . a glamorous life? No, just exhausting, often with no rest time between cities, and with a lot of plain hard work—keeping clothes in order and clean; changing in odd places before they appear on stage looking so neat and put together, creating an atmosphere of elegance to go with the wonderful music; and constant rehearsals, with travel and food and water changes affecting health as well as comfort.

Franz came back to where I was standing, having cancelled our attending the dinner. Elisabeth said that of course she understood, but that no one would want to have the dinner without our being there too, so she would come straight to the concert hall.

I have known many unrealistic dreamers who try to plan a life that will be undisturbed. They deliberately push away babies, family continuity, other interfering responsibilities, and even moral barriers in order to be "free" from all restrictions—free from any need to consider anyone other than themselves and their own pleasure and ambitions. But as Franz and I walked back to the piano, and as I sat there beside it, contrasting the candle-lit restaurant with roses on the tables and fragrant food being placed before people . . . with this empty hall and stage-hands arranging chairs and music stands . . . and watched Franz . . . I made another contrast: I watched him faithfully continuing, note after note as the minutes and hours passed. How important what he was doing would be to Van Cliburn's playing; to the orchestra in the blend of sound; to the audience in their expectant anticipation; to the conductor as he "hears" each note in his head before it all begins. I began to parallel Franz's pushing aside of other desires and special plans with a mother cancelling a long awaited evening because of her child's high fever; or a sudden trip to the hospital with a teenager's ski accident or hockey or football injury; or a round-the-clock vigil outside the intensive care unit. There are all-night meetings of Congress which cancel many planned evenings or dinners; fire fighters, Coast Guard sailors, Red Cross volunteers—they all know about cancelled plans.

Putting other people before our own tidy plans is a reality that needs to be observed by the next generation. It needs to be observed in order to be prepared for life. The lives of human beings are not guaranteed to be protected little boxes, tied up with ribbon, set aside for birthdays, weddings, vacations, dinner parties, sports events, marked, "DO NOT DISTURB."

Even those who choose hedonistic freedom, who set out to live totally selfish lives, find unpredicted disturbances spoiling their dreams and plans. And *they* never know the counterbalancing satisfaction of having stuck to a job or a responsibility that has positively affected another person's life. There is a priceless reality worth working for in sticking to a task, doing well, fulfilling promises, striving for great results in our

work. Is such commitment costly? Yes! But it is also
rewarding.

There is movement now at the front of the hall and we see two
very distinguished, stunning women, beautifully dressed, walking
in with Van Cliburn and another fine looking man. They are
Mrs. Susan Tilly, president of the Van Cliburn Foundation, and
Dr. and Mrs. Medilino of New York and Rome. Dr. Medilino is a
gynecologist in New York, and Mrs. Medilino is an interior
decorator as well as mother of three adult children, living and
working in Italy. As we all meet and exclaim over our expectations for the concert and our pleasure in hearing Van Cliburn
again, Franz and the others begin to reminisce over concerts past.
Anecdotes are related about France, Italy, New York, and Texas.

Van Cliburn is friendly, and effervescent in his enthusiasm. I
had been remarking that the ten basses looked like a frozen
ballet standing along the side of the stage. Suddenly all those
basses came to life as the musicians began to file in for the
rehearsal—each one picking up his or her instrument, immediately beginning to bring forth a mixture of conflicting sounds,
each ear hearing only his own sound, each one concerned with
the tuning of his own instrument. Yet all these instruments
would soon be blended in just the right mixture of timing and
sound, of crescendo and diminuendo, when the baton of Mariss
Jansons was lifted.

Mr. Jansons is Music Director of the Oslo Philharmonic, and
Associate Conductor of the Leningrad Philharmonic. His history
of conducting would include names of some of the greatest
orchestras in the world, including the Cleveland Orchestra. He
also has recorded all the Tchaikovsky symphonies for BBC
Television. Yet no matter how well anyone has conducted,
played a bass, blown a trumpet, tuned a piano, played a
Tchaikovsky solo on the piano; no matter how outstandingly
someone has played tennis or hockey for that matter . . . in the
past . . . the immediate present is always a new challenge.

As the conductor raised his baton, the rehearsal commenced
with the Tchaikovsky Symphony No. 4 in F Major, Op. 36. The

confident burst of brass instruments, the piercing high notes of one wind instrument, the deep bass notes of others, the lighter, sunny cheer of other notes, promised a fresh treat, an exciting newness of hearing as the conductor stopped the artists, started them again, giving his commands in Russian.

Then in came Van Cliburn to rehearse his solo part with the orchestra. He walked across the stage like a general reviewing his troops. Straight and tall, six-foot-four, shoulders back . . . walking with a purpose. An impressive entrance.

This was the rehearsal. In the concert that evening there would be an intermission in between the Symphony No. 4, with its grand finale, and the beginning of Tchaikovsky's Piano Concerto No. 1 in B-flat Minor, Op. 23, which Van Cliburn would be playing. The entrance in the evening would be even more impressive, in full evening dress; and the stage would be rearranged during the intermission. During the actual concert, the intermission would give time for the proper changes to be made.

As musicians filed out into the halls and looked into the big dressing rooms lined with mirrors and shelves, they also looked at the open wardrobe trunks along the wall, searching for their names—"Hukumum, Mopozab, Puoikug"—each box-like cubbyhole with shoes (socks stuck in each pair!), a hanging cupboard on the other side of the open trunks with rows of black jackets, a shirt hanging under each one, names for quick identification. In the next few hours all the orchestra members, the soloist, the conductor . . . and all the audience as well . . . would be dressing, would be transformed into a formal state.

But at the more informal rehearsal, as Van Cliburn came to take his place at the piano, members of the orchestra slapped him on the back and greeted him affectionately.

As you'll recall, Van Cliburn burst into world fame in 1958 when he won the first "Tchaikovsky Competition" in Moscow. He made front-page news all over the world, was given a ticker-tape parade in New York, returned to play a series of concerts in the Soviet Union, while his recording of Tchaikovsky's Piano Concerto No. 1 in B-flat Minor, Op. 23 became the first classical album to "go platinum," selling a million copies. As an international hero, Van Cliburn introduced millions to the beauty and excitement of classical music. Amazing doors opened for him as he was invited to perform around the world. And he in turn gave back, providing scholarships for young artists at Juilliard, Cincinnati Conservatory, Texas Christian University, Franz Liszt Academy in Budapest, the Moscow Conservatory, and the Leningrad Conservatory, to name just a few of his many personal philanthropies.

Right now Van Cliburn was striking some impressive chords, as the smaller orchestra was getting settled for the rehearsal. The president of the Van Cliburn Foundation was watching intently from the front row, listening and watching as she waited for the rehearsal along with Dr. and Mrs. Medilino. They nodded and whispered, making observations to each other. AP reporters, a man and a woman, were taking shots of Van Cliburn from varied positions, kneeling near the stage . . . snap, snap . . . going along the front, bending, going up one aisle or another . . . snap, snap, click, click. Reporters from various newspapers were taking notes. People scattered throughout the hall were there to listen with personal pleasure, or with a critic's interest, or from the angle of public relations for the next concert. All the seats had been sold for the night, so there was no anxiety about empty seats.

As Van Cliburn sat, back straight, hands ready to be lifted for the first fantastic beginning of his solo part, Tchaikovsky's Piano Concerto No. 1 in B-flat Minor, Op. 23, he was ready to tackle that which, when it was first written in 1875, was pronounced "unplayable."

For a moment, whoever you are, whatever is discouraging you right now, put yourself in young Tchaikovsky's place that day 115 years ago. Tchaikovsky had become a student at St. Petersburg under the young, energetic composition teacher, Anton Rubinstein. Naturally he sought Rubinstein's views on his work, and was greatly influenced by him. When he had written this concerto, he had arranged to meet Rubinstein in a classroom, to play it for him. After the first movement, not one word was said, not one word of praise or criticism. It was an agony to Tchaikovsky, but he went on playing to the end. Finally the storm broke. "The concerto is worthless!" Rubinstein said, "unplayable—passage work fragmented and clumsy beyond all salvation; trivial; vulgar . . . to be thrown away or completely rewritten."

Tchaikovsky's reaction was to publish it just as it was! And to send it to Boston to the brilliant German conductor and pianist Hans von Bülow, who gave it a world premiere in Boston, October 25, 1875, and repeated it in New York a month later. And in 1891, Tchaikovsky himself performed this concerto at one of the gala concerts opening Carnegie Hall.

Now, one hundred years later, thousands of miles from Russia and long after Tchaikovsky's death, here sat Van Cliburn, who won the Tchaikovsky competition in Moscow; there stood the conductor of the Leningrad Orchestra; and there sat German-American Franz, waiting to hear a piece of his favorite music played by one of his favorite pianists. And this was just the rehearsal. Soon there would be 2000 people, each with differing amounts of knowledge and music appreciation, each of whom would respond in his or her own way to Tchaikovsky's work. Having been condemned to the rubbish heap, this concerto has been played and enjoyed for a hundred years. Take courage, you who are working on some creative work!

Van Cliburn's fingers had now begun their rapid, precise, and powerful playing, and everyone was riveted in attention to the piano and the accompanying orchestra. There were some slow movements, some waltzing movements; Van Cliburn's awesome hands not only have an amazingly wide reach, but they fly over the keys with trills, and do wonders with the boisterous parts right up to the powerful, breathtaking close.

Now remarks were made to each other: "Brilliant!" "Fabulous!" "Wasn't it great!" The same remarks would be multiplied in the evening after the concert, and would be written in critics' accounts in newspapers. Thunderous applause and many curtain calls in the evening would give the audience an encore. Everyone hoped there would be a continuity from now on of concerts featuring Van Cliburn, and declared that he *must* keep on and not take another "sabbatical."

There is a "Green Room" in Carnegie Hall and in some other concert halls as well, where a few people are admitted to meet the soloist. At this concert there was such a variety of people waiting to meet Van Cliburn—people from different parts of his life and career: One elderly woman had known Van Cliburn's mother in New York—she had attended the same church; there were young musicians who admired him, and people from Steinway; there were people who had come from Texas to hear him, and a few who had played in the Van Cliburn Competition at one time or another. He really is a warm and friendly person, and he greeted each person kindly.

When he spoke to Franz he thanked him profusely for the splendid condition of the piano. Everything had been just right. The response to his fingers had been just what he had wanted.

You can imagine Franz was glad that he had "stayed with his patient," that he had hovered over that one new string, caring for it right up to the time when the piano was rolled out for the second half of the concert. Nothing can replace the quiet satisfaction that comes from a piece of work done well, from faithfulness in little things.

And there is no way of knowing what disaster will result when such little things are neglected!

Perhaps you remember the parable of the Talents, in Matthew 25. A man traveling to a far country gave his servants various portions of his wealth to care for while he was gone. When he returned from his journey the servants came and showed how they had increased the portions entrusted to their care. And the master said, "Well done, thou good and faithful servant: thou hast been faithful over a few things, I will make thee ruler over many things: enter thou into the joy of thy lord." (verse 21, KJV)

Faithfulness is so often not stressed, and not taught, and unhappily in this time of history is often not practiced. The difference the "few things," or "small things" have made in history may never be known to many people, but it is definitely known to the Lord of lords, the King of kings, the Master of the universe, the one true God, the Creator of all things.

The broken string at the Van Cliburn concert is a fitting place to end the story of Franz Mohr. For it is indeed the story of one man whose faithfulness in so many little things has made such a tremendous difference in so many lives.

Franz's faithfulness is simply one small part of his overall quality of character—a character as real, as genuine as the Steinway pianos he loves so much.

And that quality of character is simply a product of his certainty that the Lord of the universe is his God indeed, his Father in heaven.